The Diary
of the
Real Soul Crew

Annis Abraham Jnr

HEADHUNTER BOOKS
www.headhunterbooks.co.uk

Contents

Acknowledgements

Once again a big thank you to my wife Joanne for typing it all up and being patient with me and special love to my children Annaise and Alexandra and of course my wife.

A big thank you to all the lads who helped put it together with all their stories. Pat Dolan (Chelsea), Jonathan Evans (Cardiff), Michael Dye (Cardiff), Viking (Cardiff), Little Collin (Cardiff), Frankie D (Cardiff), Jeff Marsh (Cardiff), Simmo (Cardiff), Glenn V (Cardiff), Lee 'Tonto' Davies (Cardiff), Dave Chappell (Crystal Palace), Con (Cardiff), Paul Corkery (Valleys Cardiff), Big Sam (Valleys Cardiff), Gwyn Davies (Valleys Cardiff), Ian Thomas (Valleys Cardiff), Alex Mannings (Cardiff Youth), Stefan (Offenbach FC), Mark Gregory (QPR), Diddy (Boro), Hicky (Chelsea), Gilly Shaw (Wolves).

Martin King for making this happen and John Barnes for all his hard work behind the scenes.

A special thanks to Dave Sugarman, Vince A, Jaffa (Alun Griffiths) and also Wolf from Port Talbot for the newspaper cuttings and his 70's story about the Jacks.

Thanks Goffy, Mac, P Mannings, Ginger Jones, Rawlings, Darryl, Bradley, Dave Bennett, Jamie Sullivan, Lyndon Cushing, Cadget, Richard E, Kersy, Shep, Terry, Staples, Wally, Jeff, Joff, James, Andrew Jones, Gregson, Beer, Wheller, Big Foot, Maxwell, Richard Cordle, Ivor, Oggy, Gary S, Ginger Nick, Brummy, Webber, Gonk, Simon Williams, Julian, Rusty, Santos, Julian J, Bret, Roy Jones, Baggers, K Evans, Jason, Toddy, Kenny (Aberdare), Pricey, Dowie, Alistar, R Morey, G Price, Mojo, Dayo, Wilts, Fisher, Marksy, Stud, Ketty, Mr Williams, Sticky, Peter Morgan, Gareth (Sect A and all the other lads who sit in there), Big Tec, Little Tec, Chris Price, Craig McGowan, Vince, Matthew, Wayne (Dibs), Morgan, Leighton, Thomas, Christian, Dean, Wilbur, Lug, Chongo, Dobbo, Wilo, Gabby, Jacko, Jammo, Cissy, Mexi, Moggsy, Dulla, Derym (and all the Ely Trendies), M Lyons, Big and Little Bubble, Mark (Penarth), Dai Thomas, Harvey, Nick and Dave (Bluebirds Fly), Marco, Jock, Pam, Jermaine, Lee, Sian, Nigel Lancastle, Penny,

Dixie (Penarth), The Brownhills Dirty 30.

Topman, Catherine D, Helen Thomas, Nadia, Joseph & Sarah, Tony Dai H, Jona (Brighton), Mallo, Pocock, Spud, Richie (Blackwood), Johnny, Ben, Chris, M Gardner, Karl and Ashley from Hereford, Stan from Pontypool, Deacon, Glenn Waife, Ian Charles, Zubb, Earnie, Gee, Harry, Stanley, Sully, The Valley Commandos, The Rhondda Lads, Rotters, Woody, Nigel, Quinny, Kenny H, Wilburs, Jerky, H (Thailand), Dibble, David Stanley, Simon (Neath), Matty, Sandham, Scouse, Nigel, Gary J, AP, Anton, Phyllis (Port Talbot) and all the Bridgend lads. Pete Lintern, Mike Flyn, Lee Beames, Newt, Beefy, Bevan, Blond Simmo, Chris (Caerphilly) Carlton, Dafyd, Worzel (Gloucester), Ian (Older Blue), Jesse, Hue Boy, Robert Maggs, Emlyn and Patrick Bridgwater. Gethin and Chris (Original Soul Crew). Baker brothers, Lez, Jammo, Beards, Shoulders (and all the rest of the older Lads from Llanrumney), Mark Duddin, Rhys (Major), Brian Edge, Paul (Fairwater), Pidgeon, Ching, Jerry (Gezza), Frankie Humphries, Pill Blue, Leon & Harley Phipps, Martin (Cardiff 74), John (a true Blue in Jackland), Gazza & Peter (Bridgend), Joe Mullins, Beachy, Ducky, PVM (Port Talbot), Neath Blue, 1927 Lads, Milford Haven Blues, Holyhead Blues, The Donut Crew, North Wales Blues, Ant Hill Mobs, Chuggs & Chuggy, Jellyhead and all the lads from The Neville Pub.

To all the lads from Sunderland Brookie, Daz, Joe, The Twins and the many more Sunderland that I have met who have always made me and whoever has been with me welcome. You have always gone out to show great hospitality.

David Williams (author of Desert England), Rowland (Pompey), George Calder Kilmarnock FC, Mark Forester (Villa), Fowler and all the lads from Villa and I know the following are your arch rivals but Big Al, Bones and Cuddles from Birmingham City, whenever I have bumped into them from Dublin to Glasgow, they've always bought me a drink and made me feel welcome.

Prickett, Ian Woodruff, Adams and Dave R of Newport County, Neil of Wrexham, Muffy(Leeds Utd), Alan Swain (Bristol C), Para Paul (Millwall), Paul (Reading FC), Mike (Wigan), Murco (Stoke City), Tony Reardon (Bolton W).

RIP Derek Ford, Budgie and Ginger Jason (Cardiff C), M Rayer (Cardiff C), Manny (Bradford C), Lemmy (Newport County).

Introduction

This book is about the lads I have met over the years and who all have a tale or two to tell about their times with the Soul Crew or against the Soul Crew. They and I will all get slated by the so called do-gooders but the fact remains there was trouble at Cardiff, home and away, whether people like it or not and Cardiff through the years has had a huge mob and has always been up there amongst the very best so it's now part of history, just like everything else that happens in life.

Due to the success of my first book, 'From Shattered Dreams To Wembley Way', a lot of the lads approached me and asked if I was interested in putting some stories together. I then asked many lads who I had met over the years if they had a tale to tell and that's how this book has come about. During the last 30 odd years some of these lads have fought against the Soul Crew and against each other but as years have gone by they have developed a respect for each other and have even become good friends.

Pat from Chelsea is now one of my best mates and you couldn't ask for a better mate. He is well respected in the football world and is now a friend to many. Pat won't bullshit. He will tell you how it is whether Cardiff lads like it or not. The same goes with my good mates Jonathan and Viking who I have known since we were kids. I have the utmost respect for them. They won't bullshit one bit and will go straight to the point just like they did in their many battles for the Soul Crew.

Over the years of following Cardiff I have met some good lads and some wankers too. Dave from Palace is another true mate of mine. He won't make out to be a top lad but he's seen a lot and been involved when it matters - he will also tell you the truth.

Simmo, who is much older than me and has been around the scene a long time, is a well known character and a very likeable one at that. On many occasions when lads have tried to slag me down, he has been one of the first to stick up for me. He and his wife Pam, who is also well respected by the lads of Cardiff and other clubs, have become true friends of mine.

Three great valley lads, Big Sam, Gwyn Davies and Paul Corkery have all written a piece in this book. These lads were there in the days when the crowds were 1,500 at home and 300 - 400 away. I have a lot of time for these lads. Not only are they good lads but they are Cardiff through and through.

Now Little Collin; I've known him since my school days and we have even worked together. He's a boy and a half. One of the smallest lads you will ever meet but one of the gamest with it who would actually put his life on the line for you.

Mikey Dye is one of my old mates and we have kept mates through all these years. He is a great organiser and a great lad to be with. He has many tales to tell.

Diary Of The Real Soul Crew

Frankie Dee. I've had some right laughs through the years with him and he's always been well up for it, another good mate who I could rely on when needed.

Jeff Marsh is the author of the 'Soul Crew Seasiders' and the 'Trouble with Taffys'. I was one of the first to take Marshie to away games, a lad you could always rely on and a lad I have a lot of time for.

Con, a true gent. We go back to the early 80's, a hard lad in his day and if called upon would be there now for you. A great laugh to go away with and so organised. (Almost as good as me! He He!)

Tonto (Lee Davies). A great lad to have on your side. As game as you like and like most people in life they move on and settle down. He now follows the Welsh football team all over the world.

Glenn V. A smashing lad who loves his clothes and his football. He was never an out and out lad but paid the price for being in the wrong place at the wrong time.

Stefan (Hoffmeister) of Offenbach FC (Germany). It was unusual to have a German with us for a couple of years but he turned out to be a good laugh and he was able to take the mick out of the opposition on many occasions and even though he liked Celtic, I still like him and he always took it on the chin about Germany losing the war.

Ian Thomas. Still a youngster but a very game lad. On the many trips that I still go to, we always sit down and have a good drink and chat together and he always has a tale to tell.

Alex Mannings. Don't really know him that well but all the youth highly respect him and many of the older ones like Simmo have high regard for him.

Gregors and I go back a long way. He loves to wind up the opposition and has probably made more enemies than anyone I know but I tell it as I find it; he's always been a good lad to know through the years and a good laugh with it and probably has the most stories anyone could tell.

Diddy of Boro. Well we all know how good Boro are and, with lads like Diddy with them during the 80's and 90's, they knew they had a good firm. I met up with him at many matches during the years and Jonathan and Viking have a lot of respect for him too.

Hicky. The legend of all time. I met him when I was 16 years of age. He was one of Chelsea's top lads then and still is to this day. They've never had a better leader than him.

Gilly of Wolves has a great sense of humour. No matter how many times they've tried to bring him down or stop him going, he always appears somewhere or other but is always at the front.

One of the main faces of the 70's was a legend called Frankie Humphries and during my younger years, that's the name I always used to hear. By the 80's, Cardiff's mob took a total turn for the better and the trend changed and with it came the casual look and by '82 a lad called Parsons had come on the scene big time. For the first time ever, Cardiff became an organised force and Parsons was the one who even came up with the name, 'Soul Crew' but, as most Cardiff lads know, Parsons became too big for his boots and was sent on his way.

And so the Soul Crew which dispersed into smaller groups such as 'The Young Soul

Crew', 'Ely Trendies', 'PVM' (Port Talbot), Barry Soul Crew Seasiders to mobs from different valleys, these groups were later to be joined by 'The Dirty 30' (Docks boys and Brownhill's) who were one of the gamest firms around. By the 90's, Cardiff had probably twenty different firms and half of them not even getting on with each other. As the team declined, the different firms numbers became smaller and that eventually started to get everyone to go together again. By the end of the 90's, we even had a mob called the 'Battle Bus' and on many occasions they themselves would take up to three coaches of good lads to away games.

The Sam Hammam era created the Valley Rams and you could have anything from 5 to 15 coaches going away. Some of them were known as the Valley Commandos, unorganised but if any opposition came their way they would of needed to have had their best lads out as the Valley Commandos were virtually all the old heads from the 70's and 80's who feared no-one. Along with them and the Battle Bus mob, they were probably the biggest firm in the country during the Sam Hammam era.

The tales they are about to tell are of all their own experiences and, whether people like it or not, it's how they felt what happened at the time.

Annis Abraham Jnr, September 2008

Chapter 1
The Raging 70's
(Pre Soul Crew days)

During the 70's, hooliganism was out of control and hooligans came from every club in the league from Cardiff to Man Utd. The 70's were different from the 80's. Fighting could go on all day in the 70's and there was hardly any segregation, no CCTV, no police spotters and, in those days, it was the fans with scarves and football tops that would be fighting.

Cardiff City were going through a bad time in the 70's on the field especially after the sale of John Toshack to Liverpool. All their fans had to look forward to was a punch-up with the opposition. Man Utd, Leeds and Chelsea had thousands of hooligans and even Rochdale, Torquay and Halifax had their own hooligan element. Cardiff was known during this period for being a mad and unwelcoming place. You knew if you went to Cardiff for a game then you had to have hundreds of nutters with you just to survive. Cardiff's mob then was never really organised. They just had thousands of lunatics who were very passionate about their team. One name who was a legend with Cardiff in the 70's was Frankie Humphries and the lads that went with him were as game as anyone. The fans we had in those days came from all over Wales and some even came from Hereford and Somerset to support the Bluebirds. If you had Welsh ancestors, then a lot of fans living all over England gave their allegiance to the Bluebirds.

At home games, Cardiff were one of the best in the hooligan world but, when it came to away games at places like West Ham, Millwall, Chelsea, Man Utd, Pompey and Leeds, we had the lads but no organisation which meant Cardiff came unstuck on many occasions.

I started supporting the City in the middle of the 70's and, as a kid coming out of Ninian Park at the end of every game, hundreds of fans would go steaming past me down Sloper Road towards the away end and all hell would break loose. As the years went by, Ninian Park became so intimidating and feared by the away fans that less and less away fans came.

In the early part of the 70's, Pompey took a right liberty when they came to Cardiff. About 300 - 400 of their lads went on the Grange End (Cardiff's end in the 70's, now split with home and away fans). As soon as the turnstiles had opened, Pompey made sure they were first in and all made their way to the back of the Grange End. As Cardiff fans arrived bit by bit, Pompey kept steaming down into them and never let Cardiff settle and get together. Pompey held their own and to this day they are the only team ever to take Cardiff's end. They were kept in there throughout the whole game with about 200 police standing in front of them.

Man Utd in the '74/'75 season had run riot everywhere. They had gone and taken over everywhere they had been. The Red Army as they were known came in their thousands to Cardiff and boy did they need them, everyone of them. Cardiff wasn't going to be a soft touch like the rest. That day, we came down from the valleys in our thousands; some even the night before. From early morning that day on every street corner stood the lads from all over Wales. There were running battles everywhere. Every train that arrived was attacked and, as soon as they walked out of Cardiff Central, the Valleys were like vultures and never let the Red Army have a minute's peace. They had the shock of their lives and hadn't been used to such numbers attacking them before. Cardiff were never going to let their city be taken over by them. The Valleys had been dreaming of this fixture the minute Man Utd had been relegated from the old Division 1. All the way down to Ninian Park, Cardiff lay in wait and Utd had to battle their way through.

Both sets of fans battled all the way through the match and gave as good as each other. After the game, Cardiff continued to attack them from Ninian Park to Tudor Road to Cardiff Central Station. The Red Army had never before left a city in such a hurry and those that escaped unscathed were the lucky ones.

St David's day, March 1st 1975, Old Trafford - The Return. 4,000 Cardiff were allowed to make the trip and everyone was expecting the biggest backlash ever after what happened at Ninian Park. Somehow, it was a total anticlimax. Firstly, Cardiff didn't have the thousands of hooligans that everyone thought would travel and secondly, Utd weren't as mad at home as they were when they were going away. Cardiff were quite a young firm and Utd on the day did have large gangs roaming around but, from the beginning, the police had the situation well under control. Those that went said it was still a very intimidating place but it couldn't be compared to how it was in the first game in Cardiff. So it ended up as practically a non-event for violence with City on the pitch getting hammered 4-0.

Leeds in the 70's was one of the most intimidating places to go and could be compared with Ninian Park on how hostile the home fans were to the visiting fans. 5,000 City fans travelled up there to the FA Cup and, before the game, Cardiff gave Leeds a right shock. As soon as they stepped off the coaches, Cardiff just didn't wait around to see what would happen - they just went berserk and ran Leeds everywhere outside Eland Road. Leeds were totally stunned by this. During the game when a lone Cardiff fan ran on the pitch, kicked the ball in the net, then put his scarf down in the goal mouth and kissed it, this sent the Leeds fans mental and they invaded the pitch which resulted in over 40 arrested. During the second half, fighting then erupted on the terraces and continued until the end of the game in which City lost 4-1. As the Cardiff fans came out of the away end, over 2,000 Leeds fans were waiting baying for revenge for what had happened before the game and they did get their revenge for nearly every City fan that went that day have said they received some kind of kick or punch from the Leeds nutters. Cardiff did stand and fight back but were taken totally by surprise; exactly what Cardiff had done to Leeds before the game. So, off the pitch, it was 1-1.

Chelsea? Well Cardiff v Chelsea. We have always been big rivals off the pitch for the last 40 years and, to be honest, there was so much to be written about them.

I could write a book on its own. Throughout this book with the help of Chelsea Pat, I have told many stories. Both firms have a lot of respect for each other. In 1976, Cardiff did what Leeds have only been known for and that's smash up Chelsea's scoreboard .But we went a step further than Leeds did and, after the game, Cardiff ran around to the Shed end and attacked it. Chelsea never forgave Cardiff for that and in 1977 Chelsea came down to Cardiff in massive numbers. Not only did they have big numbers, they actually outnumbered Cardiff that day and were older and better organised. By the end of the day, Cardiff had been run ragged. Cardiff had stood in the park opposite Ninian Park and did go toe to toe with them for a while but, in the end, Chelsea's numbers took their toll. On Tudor Road, Cardiff and Chelsea fought battles and many from both sides were left covered in blood but, once again, Chelsea's numbers won the day.

Spurs brought a mob for the FA Cup in 1977 but they were smashed by Cardiff and didn't even compare to what Chelsea had brought.

Millwall have never come to Cardiff in their thousands but, whether it has been 10 Millwall or 300 Millwall, they are always up for it and they don't care how many you've got, they'll stand no matter what. That has happened through the years; every time they have visited Ninian Park. One evening during a mid week game in the 70's, about 70 Millwall came down. Not much happened before the game as Cardiff hadn't been out in force but, after the game, hundreds of Cardiff waited down Sloper Road. The police panicked and tried to get Millwall into the Park opposite the ground as the fighting on Sloper Road was getting well out of control. Cardiff was repeatedly attacking the police to get at Millwall. Eventually Cardiff burst through the police lines and the police were made to scatter and, to Cardiff's surprise, Millwall just stood there. Then about 30 Millwall who were all armed with ammonia sprayed the baying mob of Cardiff. Cardiff backed off and with that Millwall ran out of the park sending Cardiff further back onto Sloper Road but then hundreds more Cardiff surged forward and steamed straight back into Millwall. All hell broke loose and the police themselves went mental and until they finally managed to get it under control. As the 70 Millwall were being escorted by the side of the Ninian Park pub, Cardiff attacked again and again. To be fair, Millwall were themselves fighting the police and some even getting through as most of the police were facing Cardiff. Those that pushed through received a right hammering due to the numbers of Cardiff.

As the streets were now totally in darkness the fighting became worse. For over half an hour the police had to battle with both mobs who were intent on getting at each other. By the time Millwall had returned to Cardiff Central, behind them was over a mile of debris with windows, cars and anything that had got in the way, smashed to pieces in the attempts to get at Millwall. When Millwall left that night, they left with Cardiff having a lot of respect for them. Not once did Millwall cower; they had been up for it just as much as Cardiff, the only difference was that night Cardiff had the numbers.

I've been told time and time again that the early 70's in the hooligan world was mental. Well, here are stories from the middle of the 70's right up to 2007. See how they compare to those days and these stories are told by some of the top lads in football.

December 1975 Millwall v Cardiff City By Paul Corkery

We had travelled to London on a coach from the valleys. There were three coaches in a small convoy and we arrived near the ground. It was always a daunting trip going to Cold Blow Lane in those days. This third division match was to be one of the most terrifying. I was sixteen. Most fans on the coach were of the same age apart from the organisers and a couple of old people down the front. We pulled up near the ground. Outside, a shell of a burned out terraced house, a racist motivated arson attack, had killed some of the occupants a few days earlier and the atmosphere amongst us changed from banging on the coach windows and 'flashing the V's' to passers-by to a sudden realisation that this was not a normal away trip.

A few minutes later, the three coaches turned into a sort of wasteland/car park area and two Millwall nutters run at our bus banging on the side, frothing at the mouth like rabid dogs. A copper with a dog chased them off. We stepped off our coaches and were glad to get inside the ground. We were in a corner with a floodlight pylon blocking part of the view. There were about 6,000 inside the ground with almost 300 from Cardiff. We had a small seated area to our left that run the length of the ground. The rest of the stadium was terracing and there was very little signs of fences or police inside the ground. There was a thin line of coppers to our left providing some sort of barrier from the home fans. The vast majority of Millwall lads seemed to be behind the opposite goal or on the terrace near the half way line.

Millwall chanting in those days was a haunting dirge, "We are Milllwallll", "We are Milllwallll". I can't remember the other chant they kept blasting out, maybe it was "Cum on you lions" Whatever it was, I can remember thinking to myself "what am I doing here".

The match was underway and we soon took the lead, much to the annoyance of the home fans. We then went two up and then our captain Phil Dwyer accidentally poleaxed a Millwall player. Suddenly from the seated area, a Millwall fan ran onto the pitch and tried to punch Dwyer. Fortunately Dwyer is a big bloke and no harm was done before the stewards dragged the fan off the pitch. The atmosphere was getting alarmingly scarier by the minute and it appeared to me that the Millwall fans were congregating closer to us. The thin line of coppers looked a poor defence to me and I started looking around at our fans. I counted about 40 who would maybe be able to hold their own. There was another 100 or so around my age and the rest were families or old people.

Fifteen minutes into the game and unbelievably we score again. It's now 3-0. The excitement of the goal was short-lived as the Millwall fans behind the opposite goal had now moved to the side of the ground and were heading towards our end. I can't remember if there were any fences at the Den but, if there were, they were not very good and slowly but surely the growing mass of angry fans was making their way towards the thin line of coppers, like a knife through butter they steamrolled their way towards our small section. A mass brawl broke out and luckily for us there was a lot of confusion. Cardiff punching Cardiff and Millwall attacking Millwall. It was chaos and the police were powerless and outnumbered but did manage to get some fans into the relative safety of the seated area.

We were forced outside the stadium where the fighting continued and the police had more numbers but we were trapped by the turnstiles and were forced to climb over a spiked fence. I was helped over and I looked back on a scene of flying boots and fists and people bleeding and being knocked out. The police were vainly waving truncheons around trying to break it up. There were about 50 of us outside now and there were 5 lads the other side of another fence calling us. Me and my mate climbed over and joined them, thinking it was the best option ... wrong. There were 7 of us and we were isolated from the rest who had been forced in the other direction by the police reinforcements. On the other side of this fence were the Millwall fans. They spotted us and we run towards a small wall, a large hedge was behind the wall, perfect cover...we headed towards that with a mass of Millwall lads now in hot pursuit.

Without a thought, I cleared the wall with the other lads, almost head first into the bushes. Unfortunately for us, they were not bushes but the tops of trees and we plummeted through the branches to the floor, twenty odd feet below into a blackberry bush and brambles. Five of us were on the floor, stunned, bruised and covered in blood, leaves and thorns. We looked at each other and laughed. Fuck me, that was close. Above us, we could hear laughter; it was the Millwall lads, peering over the top, laughing at us.

We were in the grounds of a big house and we headed towards an open window and climbed in. We were unsure if the Millwall lads were still behind us. It was a hospital and a porter asked us what we were doing. We explained and he took us to his office. We had no idea of the score or how we were going to get back to the coach. Time was moving on and we decided to draw lots to send one of us back to let people know where we were. Hopefully the coach would pick us up. A tall, skinny kid lost and he was charged with getting back to the Den alone and sorting out our rescue. Twenty minutes later, a Cardiff fan came into the Porters Lodge. I knew him from Merthyr. He said we had to go with him back to the coach. He had a Millwall scarf on, acquired from a victory some of the lads had won against some Millwall earlier, probably the only victory off the field that day.

There were seven of us again and we walked quietly towards the stadium. It was quiet outside walking through the terraced streets but you could hear the crowd inside the Den. There was still ten minutes left of the game so we needed to hurry back before it finished.

We could see where the coaches were parked now and there were six or seven police horses by them and riot vans and lots of police. We were less than 200 yards from them when a large gang came around the corner with the police forcing them in our direction. We kept walking with our heads down and then they spotted us and a roar went up, "it's fucking Cardiff". They were sandwiched between us and the police. Luckily not all of them realised who we were so we ran straight through them. We received another few clips but some of us managed to punch a few of them and suddenly we were in front of the cops with their truncheons in hand, wondering who we were. They pushed us behind them and formed a shield around us. Next thing, we were outside our coach. It was like a scene from M.A.S.H. with bloodied bodies and people in bandages all telling their tales of the day. We found out later that we had won 3-1.

I'll Never Forget The Bob Bank At Ninian Park
By Steve Hicky Hickmott (Chelsea)

In the 70's & 80's, Hicky of Chelsea was, in the hooligan world, one of the top names in football. His nickname was 'The General'. He now lives in the Philippines and gave me his story on his way to see Chelsea v Man Utd in Moscow. Here, he tells about a visit to Ninian Park which he says he will never forget.

I was born in 1955 in Kent.

First game; Chelsea 1965/66, Chelsea 5 v West Ham 5.

Biggest Thrill; Chelsea winning FA Cup against Leeds 1970 2-1 and also taking The North Bank ARSENAL more than once.

Biggest disappointment; losing to the Yids (Spurs), FA Cup Final 1967 and League Cup Final 2008.

Nicked; Ipswich Away '72 (fined), Sheffield Utd Away '74 (3 months detention centre), Liverpool away (suspended sentence), Birmingham away (6 months prison), Villa away (fined), Spurs home (fined).

Not Guilty; Spurs away '72, Arsenal away '72, Millwall home '76, Cambridge away '78, Birmingham away '81, Villa away '81, Scotland '82.

In 1986, I was nicked for affray and charged with conspiracy at Birmingham, Everton, WBA and Chelsea home games. I was sentenced to 10 years plus 5 years to run concurrent, served 3 years 10 months and released on appeal due to police fabricating evidence in November 1989.

In 1991, I moved to Thailand and have been living there and now the Philippines ever since. I was part owner of 'The Dogs Bollocks Bar', Pattaya, Thailand 1996 - 2002 where I have enjoyed the company of loads of Cardiff City lads over the years including some who were on the Bob Bank that day.

It was the beginning of the 70's and it was the 'Watney Cup'. Cardiff were at Stamford Bridge and we (Chelsea) hadn't played them for years. The cheeky bastards had arrived early around 11:00am and they had taken over the Britannia Pub opposite the Britannia entrance. They had blue/white/yellow scarves; same colour as us. I thought they were Chelsea until we heard their accents. There was about 150 - 200 of them. Not a big firm in those days but big enough to surprise us and three weeks before the season got going.

We had enough lads for our first attack. At around 1:00pm, there was no Old Bill as nothing was expected to happen. So, with no police intelligence in the good old days, we were able to attack the pub. We steamed into them from two directions along Fulham Road and up Britannia Road; plenty of bottles and glasses were thrown and the odd punch but the fuckers stood firm outside the pub. We needed more and luckily more and more of our lot kept coming. The next attack had them on their toes trying to get back into the pub. Some sprinted away to safety. Others were caught and battered. Then the Old Bill arrived and pushed us back while they escorted the Cardiff mob into the North stand end of the ground where, in those good old days, there was no segregation. So we followed them in and took liberties. Throughout the game, we battered them. Finally towards the end of the game, the Old Bill had finally took control of the situation, put them on their coaches and sent them packing.

It was the 20th October 1979 and it was Cardiff away in the old Division 2. We left Tunbridge Wells (Kent) early and picked up lads at Bromley, Lewisham and outside Stamford Bridge. 60 lads on a 45 seater coach - those were the days. Cider drinkers, glue sniffers, dope heads and nutters, the M4 hear we come but not before we had stopped and robbed an off licence for a large amount of alcohol. Cardiff hear we come !!!!

The plan was to meet up with 2 other coach loads from other parts of London and get into Cardiff and kick the shit out of them. We arrived around 2:00pm with no police escort. We could see the ground in the distance so we disembarked and headed towards the ground and the Cardiff end - THE BOB BANK. We met a few more on our march to the ground. There was now around 80 - 100 of us, all of us lined up at the home fans turnstiles. We had agreed no talking. We didn't want them to know we had arrived. We would have soon been sussed out with our accents and that could have fucked up our surprise. We entered in an orderly fashion and gathered at the top corner of the Bob Bank towards the Grange End which is a huge side terrace. We looked around for the other Chelsea lads that had agreed to meet us at 2:30pm. Where were they? Fuck it, I thought, let's just do it now. We headed across the terraces about half way down and the chant went up, "Chelsea Agro, Chelsea Agro". We got stuck into the Cardiff lads on the edge of the main mob. There must have been between 2,000 - 3,000 lads on this end. At first, as we were laying into them, they tried to back away but the sheer weight of their numbers stopped them backing off and they stood and fought us and then fucking hell, they came down on us from everywhere and a huge row broke out. Chelsea fans on the far end and the other side of the ground were chanting "Chelsea Agro" and "North Stand, North Stand, Do your job". It was coming well on top now as we were getting battered down the terraces fighting for our lives. Their whole mob now descended upon us. We were smashed to fucking pieces and were now backing off or in some cases running for our lives. Where's a copper when you need one? We tried to regroup at the top left corner but it was all too late. We needed reinforcements but there weren't any. We were fucked.

Cardiff now had surrounded about 30 of us. Already battered and bruised in that top corner, they just came at us once again. We had lost all the other lads and hundreds of Cardiff were now at us. Some of our lads went over a wall at the back of a huge sloping drop to the place where we had entered. Down there were more Taffys kicking the shit out of us as we fought our way back to the turnstiles (a fucking disaster). At the front of the Bob Bank, my mate, Melvin, who had been beaten to the ground was now on a stretcher at the side of the pitch covered in blood. The stretcher bearers stopped at an open gate to the terraces where upon Melvin jumped off his stretcher, went through the open gate and back into the baying mob of Taffys on the terraces. This was a fantastic sight. All of the Taffys running from one nutter. Then the Old Bill took over, hauled him out and put him back on the stretcher and into safety on the Chelsea end where around 2,000 were still chanting "Chelsea Agro". Chelsea won the game 2-1.

Before the final whistle, there was no police to hold us in the ground so we just piled out onto the surrounding streets looking for the Cardiff firm. As we rounded a corner, we could see hundreds of them chanting and running towards us. They were on the grass in a park and there was a 3ft high metal spike-topped fence between us and them. We took the fence out of the ground and we charged towards their mob using it as a huge battering ram. Fights broke out on all sides but we had the metal spiked fence and used it to back them off, the rout had started. Cardiff were now in full flight across the grassy park in all directions. Some of them tried to fight back but the full force of their original attack had been broken and now the chant of "Chelsea Agro" could be heard. All the way to the train station you could hear "Chelsea Agro". A few times, Cardiff made the odd stand but it didn't last long. We arrived back at our coaches while the rest went for their trains. As we stepped onto the coaches, we realised that we had lost badly on the Bob Bank that day; outside we were the more organised and better fighting force on the streets of Cardiff.

Thanks for making it a great day to remember.

Hicky

The Tales Of The 70's by Pat Dolan (Chelsea Pat)
Firstly I'd like to say thanks to Annis for asking me to give my views and horror stories involving CCFC. I have lots of good mates at Cardiff and they have always made me welcome. They are genuine people and straight as an arrow. If they don't like you, you'll fucking know it!!!

Over the years, I've fought against the Soul Crew and the Bob Bank Boys as they were known to Chelsea and QPR. I've gone to Millwall v Cardiff with some Millwall mates and watched two huge mobs kill the Old Bill trying too get to each other and I've also been the guest of the Soul Crew in later years. The friends I've made - they are mates for life and friends come before football. I'll tell the stories about when we have been run by Cardiff and also chased after Cardiff and I'll tell it as I saw it so, if you don't agree with me, in Mickey Francis words "write your own fucking book".

When I first started going to football in the mid 70's with my father, he took me to QPR my local team. He wouldn't take me to Chelsea my own team because, in those days, Chelsea and Man Utd were always in the papers causing trouble, wrecking cities, etc....

After a year or so I started going to football without my father but instead with my mates from the street to see QPR. With my dad, I used to stand behind the goal but I now moved to the back of the loft end and, when I used to sneak off to the Chelsea matches with mates, I'd stand at the back of the Shed.

The first time I came across Cardiff was in the League Cup at a night game at Loftus Road in the late 70's. We were all standing in the Loft End when we heard a chant from the South Africa Road which is the road which runs parallel to the stadium. "CAYARDIFF" was the chant as maybe 1,500 fans came running down the road. All the QPR ran across the Loft into the part that overlooks the South Africa Road, "WE'RE THE LOFT BOYS, WE'RE THE LOFT BOYS, WE'RE THE LOFT BOYS, SHEPHERD'S BUSH" was our chant. "WE'RE THE BOB BANK, WE'RE THE BOB BANK, WE'RE THE BOB BANK, NINIAN PARK" came back from the Taffys. The Taffys had maybe 2,000 fans in the away end and maybe 50 came on the Loft that night but they were soon chased off. "RANGERS AGRO" plus "YOU'LL NEVER TAKE THE LOFT" was the QPR war cry. After the game, there was murder. All the QPR left the Loft and gathered outside the Springbok pub on South Africa Road; maybe in a 600 strong firm. Out came Cardiff and from the ground all the way up the old White City Station Road to White City Underground station, there was non-stop running battles. You couldn't say who was the winner. "WE'RE THE BOB BANK", "WE'RE THE LOFT BOYS" were the rallying cries from both firms.

The next time I came across Cardiff was with my lucky brother Johnny (or not so lucky). My brother Johnny had been to seven matches and every one was a fucking riot. To this day, he will never step inside a football ground because of what happened. Briefly, his first game was QPR v Bradford City in a League Cup game on a Tuesday night, mid 70's. Bradford brought about 3,000 fans and maybe 1,000 hooligans outside the ground. There was massive fighting and it went away from the ground and past the greyhound stadium, past White City Underground station, all the way down to Shepherd's Bush Green. Charge and counter charges as hundreds and hundreds on both sides attacked each other. Where we were stood, it looked like QPR had the better but if Bradford lads disagree I wouldn't argue as we were kids.

The next one was Arsenal v Chelsea at Highbury and, as my brother liked Arsenal, my old man insisted I take him on the North Bank. Bad fucking move. As soon as the teams came out, we realised Chelsea had half of the end and it was fucking murder. It seemed like the whole end was fighting. Chelsea never took the end but they took about a third of it. We were beaten that day 5-2 and I was beaten when I returned home because my old man thought I took him in the North Bank because I knew there would be trouble (you can't fucking win, can you ?)

The next time was Chelsea v Cardiff in a night game (I was told to stay in the ground after the game and wait for everyone to leave before we left just to make sure that, if there was any trouble, we would miss it). Anyway, in the ground, rumours were going around that Cardiff had done Chelsea outside the Britannia pub opposite the North Stand (away end). A Chelsea fan had been stabbed. As you can imagine, we didn't need any encouragement to stay inside the ground at the final whistle. After the stadium had emptied, we left and walked towards Fulham Broadway Tube station. As we entered the station, we saw a mob in green fight jackets, skins, punks etc (I think the year was '78). All of a sudden, "I'll give you a C EEE,AAA,RRR,DDD,III,FFF,FFF, CAAAAYAARDIFFF." I shit my pants there and then. My poor brother was on the verge of tears especially as he was wearing a Chelsea scarf for safety after what had happened at Arsenal. We managed to get onto the bridge that splits the platform from the central London bound trains to the trains that run south to Wimbledon. Cardiff then came piling through. "We hate cockney and we hate cockneys," was the chant as they boomed down the stairs. All of a sudden from behind them, I saw a few black faces pushing up quietly behind, then I heard the roar "WE'RE THE NORTH STAND, WE'RE THE NORTH STAND, WE'RE THE NORTH STAND, STAMFORD BRIDGE." Cardiff ran down the stairs with Chelsea behind them but fair play to Cardiff, they made a stand half way up the platform. As about 30 Cardiff stood, the rest came running back down the platform and a classic toe to toe took place on the platform which spilled onto the train. When the doors shut and the train pulled off, well fuck knows how it did, the train must have been rocking all the way to Paddington.

My brother who was now in bits swore never to go to a football match ever again. I said "Johnny, you're fucking lucky, you should go every week, you're a walking lucky charm for a punch up." Ha, ha.

The journey to The England v Wales game at Wembley in May 1981.

As the Welsh fans made their way up the M4 towards London, the Jacks, on a very rare occasion following the Welsh team, had decided to take a coach from the Town Hill area of Swansea and have a pit stop at the Leigh Delamere Service station. A coach from the Sandfields Estate in Port Talbot about 7 miles from Jackland but staunch Cardiff fans went into the same service station. As their coach pulled into the services, they noticed this Jack coach with Welsh Dragon flags on the windows and the coach operators name from Town Hill. As most of the Port Talbot coach was full of Bluebird nutters, they decided to hunt these Jacks. They soon spotted this crowd coming from the shopping area inside the services, some with Jack tops on, so they started wading into this first lot. The Swansea boys held firm for a couple of minutes but started fleeing back into the services food area with the Port Talbot lads chasing them in hot pursuit. A few of the Jacks even ran into the services kitchen quarters to escape but still took a kicking inside the kitchens. Suddenly Old Bill sirens could be heard outside. The Port Talbot lads started making a move back to their coach. Several Old Bill vans and cars arrived and started questioning a lot of people around the services whilst they held the coaches and stopped the lads leaving .Next thing you know, a sneaky little Jack was led onto the Port Talbot coach by a few coppers and was picking out several of the lads who were then taken off and arrested. Five later ended up being charged and a Camper van and a car which were also smashed up by some of the Cardiff juniors belonged to the Jacks as well.

The Port Talbot coach load must have been an ugly sight to the Jacks as it held nutters from one of the toughest Council estates in West Wales. On board that day were Jaws (now RIP), Ducko and two lads who are now serving life for murder as well as a lot more known faces. A good few Jacks were left licking their wounds after that one and it must have been so embarrassing for them.

Later that night at Wembley, the lads that were there supporting Wales were virtually all from Cardiff and from the beginning to the end of the game had to battle for their lives against the English. After the game, the odds were totally stacked against Cardiff and a lot of lads took some bad hidings.

This is a true account and has been given to me by a very old head from Port Talbot and every Jack will know this is true. What hurt the Port Talbot lads most was the Jacks being GRASSES.

10 in court for trouble at international

City, Cardiff soccer fans are fined £295

MAY 1981

FINES TOTALLING £295 were imposed by Swansea magistrates yesterday when three city fans and six Cardiff City supporters came before them charged with offences before, during and after Saturday's Wales-Scotland match at Vetch Field.

Martin David Trick, aged 17, a sheetmetal worker, of Cadle Place, Portmead, was said by Mr. Simon Rowlands, prosecuting, to have been involved in a fight between Swansea and Cardiff supporters on the North Bank of the Vetch.

Police went into the crowd, saw Trick punching and kicking in all directions, and arrested him. He was fined £50 and bound over for 12 months in the sum of £50, having admitted using threatening behaviour.

Hugh Eaves, aged 19, of Penrhiw Road, Morriston, was similarly dealt with when he admitted a similar offence. He was said by Mr. Rowlands to have been in a group on the North Bank surging towards Cardiff supporters. Told to behave, he persisted.

A similar fine and binding-over was imposed on Paul Lloyd Peters, aged 24, of Clifton Hill, Swansea, who admitted threatening behaviour.

He was said to have chased after a group of Cardiff fans, inciting others to follow.

Christopher O'Carroll, aged 20, of Tre... ...y, Cardiff... ...itted being ... Helen's ... match. ... said M... £15. ... Mache...

the sum of £50 for 12 months, but was not fined. He admitted threatening behaviour.

Mr. Rowlands said Fussell was seen to punch and kick a Swansea supporter in Oxford Street. In court, Fussell said: "I was getting my own back because a mate of mine was nearly blinded by a Swansea fan."

John William Carpanini, aged 21, of Pont Newynydd, was similarly dealt with. He admitted threatening behaviour. He was seen kicking a Swansea fan in the stomach.

A fine of £100 was imposed on Martin David Davies, aged 18, of Gelli Pentre who admitted threatening behaviour. He was bound over for 12 months in the sum of £50. He was seen shouting and gesturing at Swansea fans from the North Bank.

Stephen Edwards, aged 22, of Llantwit Major, who admitted being drunk and disorderly in Dillwyn Street, was fined £15. For a similar offence in the same area, Christopher Paul Durham, aged 20, of Dinas Powys, was also fined £15.

A tenth defendant, Dennis Brian ...

Rival soccer fans stage service-station battle

PORT TALBOT (COACH) MAY '81

WELSH soccer fans on their way to Wembley for the Wales v England international staged a pitched battle at an M4 service station causing more than £1,000 worth of damage.

Rival fans from Cardiff and Swansea wrecked two plate-glass windows and doors of the Leigh Delamere service station, 26 miles from the Severn Bridge.

Police at Chippenham investigating the incident said fighting between the Welsh fans broke out at around 5 pm, on Wednesday after two coaches — one from Cardiff and the other from Swansea — stopped at the station.

Customers fled from the car park as fans hurled stones at each other. Some fighting took place inside the foyer of the station but not in the restaurant.

One family of caravanners from the Midlands were caught in the middle of the fighting and their caravan was extensively damaged. One coach was also stoned by fans.

Police were quickly on the scene and six men aged between 18 and 20 were detained for questioning yesterday but were released last night. A police spokesman said inquiries were continuing.

Last night a spokesman for Granada, who own Leigh Delamere, condemned the fans behaviour.

"It was totally disgraceful," he said. "Luckily, none of our staff was hurt."

The spokesman said they would not ban football coaches from the station because of this incident but he emphasised that fans on coaches should give notice of their arrival to the service station. The parties on the coaches had not booked in advance.

"All we ask is that they behave like mature individuals not like hooligans," he said. "It was disgraceful behaviour."

Chapter 2
Members Only
Lee 'Tonto' Davies, CCFC

Growing up a few miles from Cardiff I suppose it was inevitable that I'd end up supporting the City. Some people's idea of supporting a club meant sitting at home with their football shirt on and waiting for the results on Grandstand. For me, it was all about being there and besides, back then I'd never be seen dead in a City shirt.

I started going to home games in the early 80's with my mates from school. We'd jump the train to Cardiff and use our pocket money to get into Ninian Park and I'd maybe buy a programme if my old man was flush that week. It was with these same mates that I experienced my first away game. It was Bristol Rovers and we'd already won promotion that season so it promised to be a good first away game. I was still in school at the time and I knew that if my old man knew where I was going, he would have killed me so I told him I was going to Cardiff swimming. I left the house early with my bathers rolled up in a towel, wedged them in a bush and I was off. I met up with my mates and we made our way to Cardiff. There were enough people on the train so we were able to get to Bristol without paying. We'd probably only been there about half an hour before we'd managed to buy some cheap cans of lager. We thought we were the business at an away game, drinking. Probably acting like the pissed up children that we were, it didn't take long to be spotted by the locals. It was just our luck that it happened to be a group of Skinheads. One of the group approached us. He was a massive bloke (well he looked massive to us, we were only kids) and he started bullying us, asking if we were Cardiff and taking the piss out of our accents. Then he tried to grab one of the boys. We shit ourselves and ran like scared sheep dropping the last of our beer as we did. An hour or so later on the way to the ground it was kicking off all around us. I'd seen trouble before this game back at Ninian Park. A few small fights and scuffles on the way to the ground and other fans trying to get onto the Bob Bank or Cardiff trying to get in the away end; the odd pitch invasions and missiles thrown but I'd never seen anything on this scale before and this close up. There were large scale clashes involving dozens of rival fans; ambulances waiting outside, smashed up pubs and, inside the ground, there seemed to be fighting in every area. I spent most of the game watching running battles through a gap in the stands between fans that hadn't gotten into the game. I suppose I didn't feel threatened in Cardiff because of the familiar surroundings but I did here and didn't fancy the walk back to the station. I was pretty sure at this point that if I arrived home in one piece, I'd never go to an away game again.

Things change and by the time I'd left school I was regularly doing more away games than homes; probably because it was always a lot more fun at away games.

It was about 1984 and it was around this time that I first met Annis. He was organising mini buses or cheap rail travel for the boys and this worked out great for me - cheap travel and safety in numbers. At this time, the hooligan thing wasn't my scene but when you travelled with this lot one basic rule was drilled into you from day one 'don't run'. I used to try and stay at the back and let the boys do their thing but even that began to be a buzz. Just being there and being able to read about it in the papers the next day, knowing I was part of it even in a small way. It didn't take long until I wanted more. Being at the back wasn't enough. Back then I was never first in but, once it kicked off, I couldn't help but get involved. From here on in it seemed like every ground we visited, it would kick-off with either small scuffles on the way to the grounds, fighting on someone's end or proper toe-to-toe battles with other firms. That's right, 'other' firms because by now I was part of the 'Soul Crew'.

About this time, clubs were introducing membership schemes to make sure home fans only entered the home end. If you were smart enough, there were always ways around that. It was a Sunday and we had an away game at Northampton. We'd been to another match the day before. This was something we used to do if Cardiff didn't have a game. I remember once watching the first half of a game at Eland Road and then the second half of one at the Odsel but I don't know where we'd been before the Northampton game. All I can remember is driving overnight and arriving in the early hours of the morning. When we arrived, we broke into their Supporters' shop and borrowed a pile of blank membership cards. We left everything else so I doubt if anyone even noticed we'd been there. We found a local phone book and filled out the membership cards with names and addresses. All that was left now was to wait for the train to arrive and hand them out. When the train arrived, we gave them to anyone who'd take them. The plan was to get as many of us as possible into Northampton's end while it was my job to go into the Cardiff end and get a mob together there. It was planned for half-time. We were going to cross that stupid bowling green they used to have at the County ground (we'd already been in earlier that morning and opened a gate at the back of the away end) and onto Northampton's end but things didn't go as planned. Firstly only about half a dozen had managed to use the fake membership cards. From what they told me later, they were given a hard time by Northampton. They had their feet stood on so they couldn't move, their hands were held behind their backs and they had cigarettes stubbed out them. Unfortunately, there was nothing they could do except wait for half-time and for us to arrive. On the stroke of half-time, about a hundred and fifty of us squeezed through the small gate and onto the bowling green only to find the police were one step ahead of us and were lined up on the far side. The presence of the Old Bill was never a problem so we ran towards them. As I moved closer, they didn't look too concerned that a hundred and fifty lads were about to attack them and, when I looked behind, I realised why. I'd looked back just in time to see the last Cardiff fan disappearing back through the gate, leaving just two of us to have a go at the Old Bill. I certainly didn't fancy our chances. I don't remember or didn't see what happened to the other lad that stood but I was knocked to the ground and literally trampled on by the Old Bill as they ran over me to try and make a few arrests. I was dragged across the grass by to the edge of the pitch by a fat old sergeant who was sweating and wheezing by the time he'd pulled me off the bowling green. All he could manage to say when he handed me over to a young copper was 'here'. When the sergeant went back to try and make a few more arrests, the young copper asked me what he was supposed to do with me. I told him the fat bloke had said I had to be put back in the Cardiff end. I couldn't believe my luck when he did exactly that. What a result !

After the game and outside the ground, it was mayhem. Running battles with the police while all the time trying to get at Northampton. It was at this time that I had another run in with my fat friend from the bowling green. Luckily he didn't recognise me. As usual, the Old Bill managed to get on top and eventually managed to get Cardiff onto buses and drove them back to the station. A few us of managed to avoid the laid-on transport by using the usual blag that we'd driven up and the car was in the car park - for once, it was true. When the buses were on their way with a police escort, we spotted a small group of Northampton calling us up a side street away from the Old Bill. We didn't need to be asked twice and ran straight into them. Our numbers were pretty even and they gave it a good go but eventually we started to get on top and they started to back off. One of their boys though was keen as mustard and wanted a one-on-one with me so we made our way into another side street while the boys ran the rest of Northampton's mob. Once we were alone, he put his hand in his back pocket and told me he was going to cut me. Obviously I wasn't too keen for this to happen but I was in no mood to run either so I told him to go for it. Sometimes it gets you like that. You know if you think about it, you'd have it on your toes but if you don't think or ponder then there's no fear, just the buzz. He pulled out his blade and I just looked at it with a smile on my face. To this day, I don't know what an illiterate moron like him was doing with a biro at a football match but that's what he was waving at me and, by the look on his face, I knew he'd pulled out the wrong tool. While he was looking at what he was holding, I took my chance and went for him. He took a couple of good blows before he went down but, in all fairness, what with firmly keeping hold of his pen in one hand while trying to find his knife with the other, he didn't put up much of a fight. It was at this point that the police made an appearance. The sound of sirens was getting louder as the van headed towards us. Now it was time to run. As I was having it on my toes, I looked behind to see if the Old Bill were giving chase. Luckily they were too busy picking up my new friend off the road and putting him in the back of their van. A concealed weapon at a football match - now there's a naughty boy who wouldn't have been sleeping in his own bed that night.

I hadn't had much experience with knives at the football. I certainly never carried one myself. One incident that has stayed with me until this day happened at Leyton Orient. It was the hundredth anniversary of the FA or something and there was going to be a mini tournament at Wembley with every team's last five league results taken into account to decide who qualified. Cardiff only needed a draw at Orient. Needless to say we were stuffed 4-1 or something and that was the end of that. At the final whistle, Orient managed to get onto the pitch so obviously we tried to do the same. I managed to get on but the police and stewards stopped most of the others. I was hardly likely to have a go at Orient on my own so I tried to blend in and find my way out of the ground. While still on the pitch, three lads came over to me and I thought bollocks, now I'm fucked. Luckily they were Cardiff and had recognised me. We decided to stick together and get out of there as soon as possible. When we were out of the ground and on the street, these three lads (who to be honest, inside the ground seemed like they wanted to be on the first train back to the Valleys) went mental. Anyone who looked like lads were having it. These three didn't give a shit. Almost the second we exited the ground, they ran straight into a mob of about thirty. By the time I knew what was happening, they'd had a kicking. The police had turned up and they were already fighting with the next lot of Cockneys. By the time we approached the station, we must have had over a dozen offs. The truth is I couldn't wait to get on the train. These blokes were dangerous. The usual lads I went to football with knew what they were doing. This lot just had a death wish. We'd managed by some kind of miracle to get to the station in one piece and I thought it was all over. No chance. Not with these three around. As I remember it, there was a hill to the right of the station with a pub at the top of it. Outside this pub at the top of the hill was a tidy little firm of maybe twenty or thirty lads. Quite frankly, they could have stayed there and enjoyed their Saturday afternoon pint but no, these three lunatics decided to have a go at them and began charging up the hill with me in tow. At first, I thought we had them worried. They didn't run but they didn't come at us either. They just stood there and it didn't take long to work out why. By the time we reached the top, we were out of breath and knackered. That's what they were waiting for and that's when they came at us. Straight away, we were on the back foot and they kicked the fuck out of us all the way back down the hill. I tried to fight back but every punch I threw they must have landed ten. They were just hitting me for fun. The next thing I knew I was being grabbed around the neck and being pulled through a small gate onto some steps. These steps were a shortcut to the station about halfway down the hill and it was one of the Cardiff lads that had pulled me through and then closed the gate. I don't know why he'd pulled me through and not one of his mates. I think I'd probably been knocked out because I don't remember fighting, just being pulled to safety. Once we were stuck on the wrong side of the gate, the other two lads we were with were brought over to the gate, held there and slashed in front of us. We'd already taken a kicking and that should have been that. There was no need to cut them up as well. The way I see it, if you put yourself in a position where you're likely to get a kicking and you get one, that's your own fault. The bruises go and your eye normally reopens within a week and you should be ready for your next off by the time the next match comes around and that should be the worst it gets.

When travelling away, we always made a point of trying to get ourselves onto other peoples home ends, probably because we were always guaranteed an off even if it never lasted too long. The easiest way to do this was to just hand over your money at the turnstile, keep your mouth shut and hope for the best. This method worked more often than not and once, at Southend, it came with a bonus. When I paid to get in, I was also given a raffle ticket for a free draw that was going to take place at half-time. I couldn't believe my luck when they announced the number. I'd won a 'flymo'. I never did collect my prize though. We'd kicked off in their end before the game had started and by half-time we'd been thrown out. We had to pay a second time to get into the Cardiff end (no free raffle this time) so I figured it might be pushing my luck a bit by trying to claim my prize.

Other times getting on the home end wasn't as much fun. Away at Peterborough we'd managed to get into their seats early and were waiting to see where it went from there. Because there was a while to go before kick-off, it was pretty empty although it never really filled up at London Road. It wasn't long before the dozen or so of us were spotted and, once we were, it didn't take too long for Peterborough to get a mob together and have a pop. Fighting in the seats was always tricky so when they came at us, we just stood our ground; they were unbalanced and falling over in their haste to have a go. Even before they reached us, we had the upper hand. Then we attacked. As we went into them, I was more concerned with tripping over seats and going down than I was about the punches being thrown at me and that's when I was gassed. All I saw was a plume of white mist coming for my face. Instinctively I scrunched up my eyes and covered my face with my hands. Immediately I felt the punches and went down. I didn't know if I'd been punched to the floor or had tripped over something but what I do know is that fighting with your eyes shut and your hands cupped over your face is not a tactic I'd recommend. While on the floor, I took a right shoeing but it didn't last long. The boys had seen me go down and had come to my rescue. I took my hands away from face to pull myself up and began to open my eyes. As they opened, there was no burning sensation and as they focused, the first thing that I saw was torn newspaper over the floor. They'd done me with the old ripped up paper in the face trick. Apart from a few bruises on my back, the only thing that was really hurt was my pride. Still, you live and learn. On the bright side, it did give the boys a reason to take the piss out of me for the rest of the season.

Coppers can spoil a good day out and I'm not talking about the one's who steam in with their batons waving because, let's face it, when that happens we're all up to something we shouldn't be and probably deserve it anyway. Besides, most of these coppers are shit scared youngsters who'd rather not be in the middle of two warring firms anyway. The ones I'm on about are the arseholes who were bullied at school, probably wet their beds until they were well into their teens and have now been given a little bit of power they choose to use to spoil your day. One (of many) that I met was on a trip to Stockport. We'd just arrived and I was getting off the train and, even before my Adidas clad feet had even touched the platform, he was on me. He had me around the throat, held me up against a wall and treated me to a sly dig in the gut and growled, "I know who you are, I'm watching you." What the fuck was all that about? I was a nobody who'd never even stepped foot in Stockport before this day. The guy clearly had issues. So it was off the station and into the first pub. A few of the boys went straight to the ground and managed to get us tickets for Stockport's seats. All that was left for me to do was get pissed. That proved easier said than done. I bought my first pint and settled down while we waited for the next train to arrive with the rest of the boys. I could've only been there five minutes when my policeman friend from the station came in. He pulled me off the chair, held me up against another wall (I was getting sick of this), treated me to my second dig in the ribs of the day. Then, not content with just the physical abuse, he told me I wasn't allowed to drink, that I was banned from every pub in Stockport and, if he caught me in another boozer, he was going to nick me. So what do you do? Easy, find another boozer. At least, I managed to drink a pint in my next port of call. While I was at the bar ordering my next one, the Old Bill came in again. This time it was a different copper. He ran straight towards me and I thought 'bollocks', nicked again. As it turned out, this one was cool. He told me the other copper picked on someone like this every time a team with a 'reputation' came to town. He said he was on his way and I should hide in the toilets until he was gone. This game of cat and mouse went on all day. Eventually we arrived at the ground and into the seats and guess who turned up after about thirty seconds. He stood in front of me with his back to the game and his big size twelve's on top of mine so that I couldn't move. He didn't even let me up at half-time for piss. His reasoning was that I'd paid for a seat and I was going to sit in it. I didn't see any of the game but he ended up doing me a favour. At the end of the game, Cardiff managed to get on the pitch and have a go at Stockport's end. Once it had all died down, the only way off the pitch for Cardiff was through a corridor that the police had formed with their dogs. I might not have seen a ball kicked that afternoon but I also never had teeth marks in my leg to nurse on the way home like most of the boys. I think that was the one and only time I've been to Stockport.

Nowadays it's all too much for me. I was actually called a 'geriatric hooligan' a few weeks back and I'm only forty. In the past, they would have just locked you in the back of the van until the game was over then put you on the train home. Now, with CCTV everywhere, you can expect a knock on your door weeks or months after the event and a banning order for the same crime. Things have definitely changed. I think I'd rather sit at home with my shirt on and wait for the results on Sky.

But then again I've never been to the Liberty.

Chapter 3
The Game, Who's Interested In The Game?
Jonathan Evans, CCFC

My name is John Evans and at the present time I'm writing this for my friend Annis whilst serving another sentence. It's my eighth time now and I have done nearly 9 years behind the door. I've been going to football since I was 11 but I'm not a great football fan. In fact, I only really go for the fight.

I was brought up a stone's throw away from Ninian Park in the Grangetown and Docks areas of Cardiff. The crew that I ran with were known as the Docks Boys. My first real memories of going to football were jumping over the fence at the back of the Bob Bank and wondering how many fans the other team had brought. I was always more interested in the 'off the field' activities than the 'on field'. Being young, I had to watch the older boys from a distance but always knew I wanted to take part in what they were up to.

I can always remember Annis and the Viking and it seemed everyone knew them and spoke to them. I had to work my way into their crew and I guess the only way that I could do that was by travelling away to games with them. The first time I went with them was when I was fifteen years old. It was Hartlepool away, the first away game of the season. And it was a good start as they tried to attack us in the seats. We had a small number but we threw seats down at them and held our corner, me, Annis, Viking, Dio, Derek etc. I was hooked!

I started to go all the time then. We had our own crew now; all Docks and Grangetown lads, black and white and we stood out. We'd grown up together and fought together at football and outside football too. We had a reputation in our own city and when we came together for games we were tight knit. We would always stand and fight together because that's how we had been brought up. Never leave your mate, no matter what.

I've known Annis for years he's the Godfather to my young baby and growing up he was the best known down the football. With Cardiff having so many firms, he seemed to be the main cog that kept everyone together. We went on many trips together. I can tell you that we had fun and games at many. When he asked me to put a few stories together, I said I would be happy to. Like I've said, I've been in prison for years and missed a lot of games but the games I'm going to write about, I've been at. I've been at the sharp end of it. So if you're in the know, you'll see that I'm no mug and I'll say exactly how I saw things. It will be a genuine account and I've only asked for and given respect when I think it's been earned. Nowadays, people think it's a result if you just go to another city, get put in an escort, then go to the game. In my eyes, that's bollocks.

So this is my account of the time and games that our crew, the Docks boys, have been involved in. Cardiff's firm on our day is massive. We have mobs from all over South Wales but our crew was the main firm in Cardiff. If you meet our lot, you've met Cardiff's main firm.

Millwall 1999.

Now I'm not going to say too much about Millwall as you know their reputation but when they came to us that August '99, they came properly unstuck. They came with a firm. They didn't fuck about. They came looking for it. The Viking and I told our lot to meet in our local, The Neville in Grangetown. Millwall arrived in Cardiff early. We had a few scraps early on but nothing too major, too many Old Bill. By 2:00pm, we had a huge mob of lads at the pub - at least 600 strong. We decided to try and get at Millwall. They were in the City Centre so we had to make our way from Grangetown by going through the side streets. Trying to take a mob like that is impossible especially in Cardiff. We tried our best but were baton-charged back by the Old Bill. Planks, bricks, everything you can name was thrown at them for at least half an hour. A dozen Old Bill on horses charged at us time and time again.

Millwall were being escorted tightly by the Old Bill all the way to the ground but we still attacked their bubble. At one stage, a police helicopter landed between us in a park; what a mad sight? So no proper punches had been thrown before the game; a proper disappointment. The game itself was a bit lively as objects were being thrown back and forth plus all the usual chants. After the game, it was game on. This is what we'd been waiting for. As we came out of our end, Millwall burst out of theirs and we had hundreds ready. There's a video of our numbers and it doesn't lie. Before I go on, I've said I'll give respect when it's due and I've must give those Millwall lads a lot of it because they are the only side I've ever seen do what they did. After they came out of their end, we were both forced away from each other by the police so Millwall went back into the ground, ran along the side of the pitch and burst out of the side of the family enclosure gate. Just as I was calling our lot to go through the same gate, we met head on. The Viking, myself and Rusty went straight in, no bouncing about and all that bollocks. Their front line was smashed bad. They bumped straight into our lot. It was great. They were forced back into the enclosure and back up the stairs. As we went forward, their lads that were knocked out were left behind on the floor. The ones that weren't KO'd were hammered and were left laid on the ground as hundreds of Cardiff poured through. 14 were taken to hospital. It was proper naughty. They were dodging each other out of the way to get away from us. They were properly done. It was a good result but, like I've said, I must give them lads respect as they were the gamest London firm to come to us. Recently we've played West Ham and Tottenham.

West Ham

West Ham done fuck all, nothing. They brought about 200, drank in town with the Old Bill outside and were happy to be escorted to the ground in a bubble. They made no attempt whatsoever to look for it whereas we had bird for trying to attack them. I was nicked before the game. A rocket was fired at the police lines to try and break them and I was nicked and charged with attempted Section 18 on a copper. I received a not guilty for that charge but had 6 months for another trumped up one. Viking had four fucking years for his part after the game as Cardiff tried to ambush West Ham in Grangetown. The judge, on sentencing the boys, said it looked like a scene from Beirut. Not one punch was thrown after the game and he received four years, fucking liberty.

In the return game at Upton Park, West Ham were done and Cardiff took the piss. When I mean the piss, we run them ragged after the game, down every side street - all you could see was the backs of West Ham. Out of about a dozen battles that day, they stood about once and then they were savaged by our numbers. We must have had 500 - 600 lads who had travelled that day and some lads had never forgot the times we had been battered there in the late 70's so I reckon we finally settled the score.

Although West Ham weren't up to much at ours or away, the old ICF were undoubtedly the Governors back in the old days but times change. I guess the new West Ham aren't a patch on the old ICF and the reunion they had back in 2001 when 400 of them went to Manchester would never have been turned over.

Tottenham Hotspur

Tottenham weren't much better. In fact, all they did was sing. I'll give them credit. They have good voices. Some of them came the night before and holed up in a pub in Grangetown. The Old Bill just kept baton charging us away. On the day of the game, they done fuck all. They were put in a bubble, marched through Grangetown and were happy to stay in their escort. Again, we tried our best to attack, five attempts we made. We burst out of the side entrance of the Grange pub. I said to the boys, "If I go out first, make sure you all follow behind me." Everyone did. Spurs saw us and just started singing. They made no attempt to break the bubble. They were a proper disappointment. As I've been saying, I'll always show respect to people or lads who've earned it. Spurs never showed much at ours but they were a different animal at home. By then though, I was in prison for the game.

The game in London was a midweek game. Our lot did travel so I can say what they thought of Spurs and what they told me was they were fucking good. Both sides had over 700 boys out and Spurs were game as fuck. I don't think either side could have claimed a result that night but our lot have told me they were very impressed with Spurs. I hope they feel the same as we do because it's all about respect and they have ours as do Millwall for the part they played that day in August even though they came unstuck - I thought they were as game as fuck.

Diary Of The Real Soul Crew

Millwall Away

In the return game, we took over 800 boys to Millwall. Me and the Viking drove up. As soon as we arrived, the Old Bill were on us. I'm sure they had our mobile numbers tapped as it was proper strange. Anyway, we had no chance of avoiding the police in the mob the size that Cardiff had that day. We approached South Bermondsey and waiting there was a massive police presence which prevented any trouble. Somehow I was still nicked before the game; some bollock charge again, another night in the cells. Never mind, shit happens.

Barnsley

Another side that had a go were Barnsley. They were game. Before the match, they broke their bubble and went looking for it and I can tell you now not many firms come to Cardiff and do that. In the city centre, we had to smash our way out of our pub to get at them. We followed them down the side streets then hit them half way down St Mary's Street. They did stand but came unstuck. A few were KO'd. Myself and Rusty flew straight into them and it was a good little battle. They stood for fucking ages but eventually we backed them off after their front line was dropped. They were still game and even in the ground they tried to burst out of their end. They battled toe-to-toe with our Old Bill and many were later dawn raided for it. So fair play to them. Like I've been saying, I can only give respect when it's due and we never even knew they were coming.

Manchester United

The next one is a tricky call and I'll say that the best firm I've seen in Cardiff are Man Utd. The mob they had for the cup final with Millwall was proper naughty. They were really, really good. We had about 80 lads out ourselves. I said to Viking to forget it with them; we'd need all our crew out for this one not just a handful but what happened next lets them down. In his book, 'Men In Black', O'Neil says they did Cardiff. True, they did chase a little mob of Cardiff, no arguments there but it was none of us. When we did arrive, we chased some of them back under the bridge. O'Neil says in his book they had a result but this is stupid to claim a result. You have to at least have fought some of our top boys. As soon as we arrived, like I said, we run a few of them and that wasn't Man Utd's main firm so we're not saying that we done Man Utd.

On another occasion what isn't in doubt is that we had a naughty mob out after a home game against Wycombe. Utd had Liverpool the next day in Cardiff and they didn't want to know. Yes, they had numbers but they just stood there behind the police lines and that hooligan documentary shows us attacking the police lines to try and get to them and it wasn't just for a few minutes - we tried for hours. Utd came out of a pub, stood there and shouted a few things and then were chased and rounded up by the police. They could have done a lot more that day to get at us but didn't. We were roaming the streets all night looking for their firm. Nothing. The mob they had never left each other so that's why I say it's a tricky one to call. Yes, they have a good firm but on the day we had our firm looking for them everywhere and they didn't seem interested to come out to us.

Jeff Marsh (right) in the 80's,
author of 'Soul Crew Seasiders' and 'The Trouble with Taffies'

Tranmere away, 80's Ely Trendies drinking before the game, Jamo, Joseph,
Revy & a few lads.

Tranmere away, 80's Ely Trendies.

Cardiff Lads, 1988

September, 1988. Cardiff fans away with Wales in Amsterdam.

September, 1988. Mojo & The Barry Lads with Wales away in Amsterdam

*In the 90's during our once again bad years on the pitch.
Some Cardiff try to stop the game at Ninian Park.*

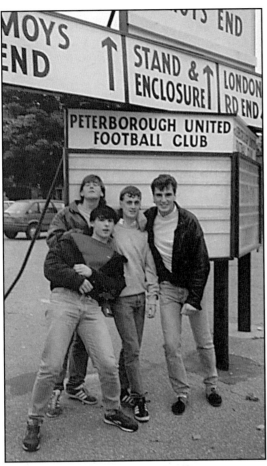

Tonto, Darryl, Mikey Dye and myself at Peterborough in the 1980's.

Boro's Mob of at least 500 on a visit to Chelsea. Boro were big during the 80's and 90's. I was there to see it myself

WITH THE football season only two weeks old, the violent face of soccer has been quick to show itself again.

The scene is Ninian Park, Cardiff, on Saturday. The victim is a young Chelsea fan, with blood pouring from a head wound, as he is attended by a policeman.

Thirty-two fans were arrested in Cardiff after the second division League match between Cardiff City and Chelsea, which the London side won 2-1.

"Many of those arrested were from London and they are accused mainly of public order offences," said a spokesman for South Wales Police in Cardiff.

Picture by ALAN GRIST

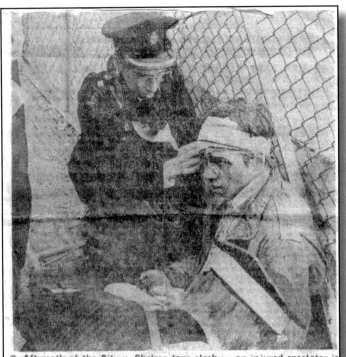

🌐 Aftrmath of the City v. Chelsea fans clash — an injured spectator is treated at Ninian Park this afternoon.

Paul Corky (Valley Rams), Gwyn Davies

Cardiff battling with the Old Bill at West Ham just after they had run the ICF at Upton Park.

The Valley Lads Housewarming party including the Old Bill.

Our main police spotter knows the Soul Crew well.
Unusual but a lot of top Cardiff lads have respect for Simon Insole.

The Valley Commandos. Just a small part of the valleys who go with Cardiff.

Some of the Cardiff lads on their way to Wrexham.

The Barry Lads who went everywhere with Cardiff in the 80's

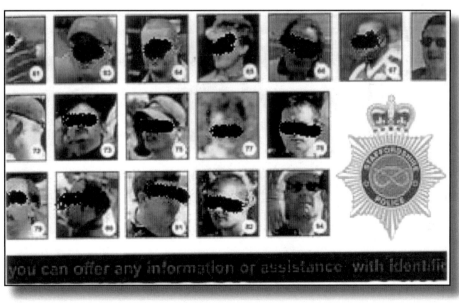

you can offer any information or assistance with identifi

Some of the many Cardiff fans wanted for Stoke away, 2000

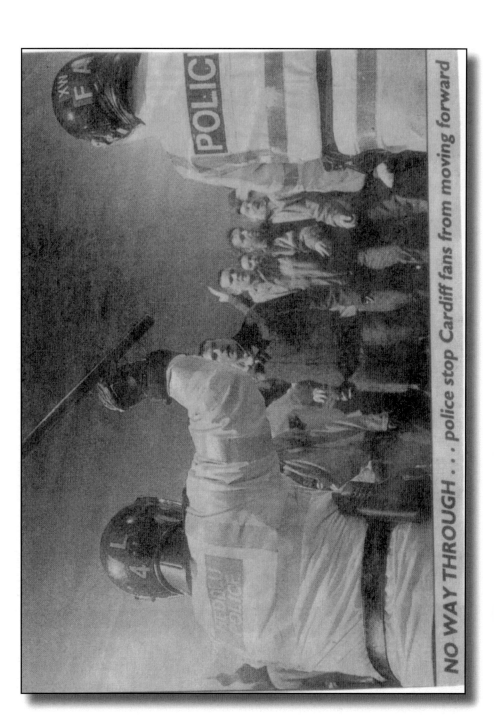

NO WAY THROUGH . . . police stop Cardiff fans from moving forward

TAUNTING . . . hate-filled Cardiff fans

Sam Hammam on coach to Mansfield with the lads, Mojo, Rawlins, Simon, etc.

The lads with Sam Hammam, Mansfield away

The Sam Hammam Champagne Army at Mansfield, 2001.
The lads with Sam & Directors at The Swallow Hotel.
Borley, Walker, Isaacs & Ronnie Bird ex-legend (RIP) player.
The lads, Simon, Twisty, Prior, Steve, Jaffa & Howard.

The Soul Crew Champagne Army, 2001 at Swallow Hotel, Mansfield.
The lads Twisty, Prior, Dai Thomas (centre), Simmons, Howard & Jaffa.

Cardiff Soul Crew arriving at Millwall

Gotcha, a cop wrestles a fan to the ground. Cardiff at Millwall

Nottingham Forest

We've got some naughty villains in our crew so it would be a good battle if we ever met head on with other teams firms like Man Utd, Chelsea and Birmingham. I've met a lot of good boys over the years especially in jail. I was once down the block in Dartmoor. I was down there for a few months on GOAD and was quite friendly with a lad from Derby. He used to tell me about the rivalry with Forest. He admitted they had a good firm so when we went to Forest, I half expected a good row. We went by cars and met in the Robin Hood on the outskirts of the city about 2 miles away. One of the boys was talking to a lad from Forest, the usual bollocks, how many have you got? Where are you? Anyway, I grabbed the phone off one of our lads and asked the Forest lad, where the fuck do you want us to go? Maid Marion Way he told me. Ok, right, we'll be there I said. We had a good mob together that day and the 70 lads there were all good faces. There was a few chats about what to do and where to go. I was in a people carrier with 7 of our lot. Viking was with me. I got us all ready and said "We're here now. It's what we've come for. They've called it on and were going."

A convoy of cars set off. We were the lead car and were approaching their city centre. As we were driving in, I could see their mob in the distance crossing the road, about 250 strong. We were clocked so I made the driver park up, bang on Maid Marion Way. Perfect, I thought. I looked around and the rest of the convoy missed our turn so only three cars pulled into the car park. I didn't give a fuck. Out we get. I walk straight out of the car park and over to Forest with the Viking right behind me. The police quickly come between us and them. With that, another mob of Forest come behind us; bang, we're over the metal barriers straight into them. There is about 15 of us, all good boys so we're not worried about numbers. As we steam towards them, they're off, backing off straight away, they have about 50 but no bottle and as we are going into them, there by the side is our police spotter, (potato head), fronting them as well. Suddenly their lumpers feel a bit brave and start bouncing around; we give it to them and it soon sends the rest packing. We're rounded up and put in a bubble. The 15 of us are marched to the ground (their papers show them covered in blood and done). We meet up with the rest of the convoy. They're gutted. They missed it but I think a few were glad they took the wrong turn. They know who they are and I've told them what I thought of them.

After the game, Forest came on the bridge and surrounded Annis, his missus and two mates; 50 onto three lads and a girl. Fuck me, that's brave. They even had his missus by the throat but thanks to Taffy Anton and his little crew (who hadn't been to the game and had accidentally been walking across the road) steaming straight into Forest and backing them off, it had prevented three lads and a girl getting a hammering. Also they knew where we were parked and the brave bastards done our windows and tyres on the cars when we were at the ground. Perfect really for us because we had to stay a bit longer. As we were standing by our cars (three cars), we started chatting to a few Forest boys. They said how good they thought we were and that they would try and bring it to us at Cardiff. As we were speaking, there was a roar from a side street and about 60 lads came steaming at us; the cunts had kept us talking whilst they got their lads together.

Diary Of The Real Soul Crew

At this time there was one copper between us so once again we went straight at them. They stopped dead in their tracks like they'd hit an invisible wall and then started to bounce around (I hate that crap). Then the strangest thing that I've ever heard at football occurred. As they backed away from us, one or two of them was saying "They're too big, they're too big." These weren't kids mind but part of their main firm. I know we have some big lads and we did that day. The Viking is 6'3 and I'm nearly 17 stone but fuck me what's all that about. It rattled my head. They didn't want to know, no bottle whatsoever them Forest lads. As for them coming to Cardiff, not a chance, total bullshit. I read that Boatsy said they had over 400. Well, they must have come as the invisible men because no-one saw a mob that size all day. They had 25 in a pub on the way into the city centre and when a car load of our lads found them and said wait hear, we'll be back, they were gone like a flash. Their big firm they talk about was no more than 80 on the train and happy to be in a bubble.

Swansea & Newport

Whilst I've been in prison, I been told about a book that Swansea have written by some clown who says he's their main man, says he's done this and done that. Why does this mug need to lie? While I'm in jail, I've met some good Swansea boys and they've never heard of you but we'll catch up one day and see what you're all about. Enough said about him for now. I'm not going to put down Swansea too much. Like I've said, I've done bird with some good guys from there and they can hold their corner. They're not out and out football boys themselves but go when needed and I do respect them. Swansea's mob though I don't rate. I do rate Newport higher than Swansea all day long especially after the battle we had in Milan with them. Wales were playing out there and it was one of the best battles I've ever had.

We flew out for the Wales v Italy game. We went with the Llanishen boys who are really good lads to have by your side. There was about 30 altogether in our little mob. On the night before the game, about 50 lads were drinking by a canal. About 25 of our lot were together; the rest were with other mobs of Cardiff but they were not with us. A lad walked into our little group clocking our numbers. I asked him where he was from, Newport he told me. Where's your lads mate? I asked him. He said they were in the hotel. OK, I thought and off he went. I said to Viking, "That cunts gone to report back to his boys, watch what happens." I walked over a humped bridge to see where he went and, within 2 minutes, out of a street came Newport's firm of about 30. They came straight over to me as I was on their side of the bridge. Hawkey, my mate went straight back to call our boys. As I was on my own now, I had a bottle on me and put it straight into the first one's chest. It started to rain bottles then. Our lot came over the bridge and then Viking went flying into their front line. It was a proper nasty toe-to-toe and, at first, Newport never budged an inch and for at least 5 minutes and I mean five minutes, they were having it.

I caught one lad flush and he went out. Viking started banging them too and Newport started to finally buckle a bit. We then all regrouped as one and charged as a unit. They wilted and backed off. Once they turned, that was it. They were smashed badly. At least three of them were hospitalised, the rest were gone, only stopping when the Italian Old Bill fired a shot. Time to get out of there but what a battle; all credit to them Newport boys.

At the same game, we bumped into the Jacks. Nothing happened at all. Too many police but that mug says different in his dribble of a book; we never threw a punch at each other. Also the mug said to me and Viking the following "We're all Welsh and it's time to call a truce." "Not a fucking chance," I said. At that point, we had over 200 boys standing there. They had the grand total of 25. Even Wrexham had a bigger mob than them so I don't know how he was nicked. He must have been pissed and the only reason why we let them go that day is because Cardiff are not bullies.

It was the Wrexham lads who kicked it off in the ground with the Italian Old Bill and then we became involved and run the Italian police out of our end. It was a proper buzz doing that but I took a few lovely cracks around my head and ear for my troubles. It's on a hooligan DVD and it shows us doing the Old Bill; it looks really good too. After the game, there was no sign of Swansea and Newport. We marched around looking for them with a good 250 boys. I like Wrexham so we don't bother with them. Another fact that needs to be sorted is that mug from Swansea had a photo taken with one of Cardiff's lads coming out of the nick in Italy. Lets get something straight. We never go with Swansea and for the first time in the last 20 years they had finally shown up at a Wales game with a feeble mob begging us to unite. Muppet.

And finally ...

To finish off my thoughts of how things have gone for myself and our band of brothers, Cardiff finally reached the FA Cup final for the first time since 1927 and I've missed it. I've missed some other big games due to either being in prison or being banned but missing an FA Cup final is heartbreaking. It seems just my luck. The reason that I'm in jail now is because I was arrested after a Crimewatch appeal which had nearly 23 phone calls naming me and the other two people I did the graft with. Grasses who are the lowest of the low.

There's been a lot said and written about the Cardiff thugs. A lot of lads rate us. Some don't. That's their right. Hopefully what I've said is seen as not a name and shame exercise. It's how I saw things and yes we have not had our own way all the time. Boro came down and had a result against us and I respect their firm a lot. I have a good rap up there and Diddy, one of their lads, has been a good friend for a long time. I've been with Boro to Swansea and I was with them for the Euro '96 Scotland game. Diddy has seen what we're all about and I'm sure he respects us.

Another team I have a lot of time for are Hull. Savo, one of their boys, is a sound guy and Hull have come to us and looked for it. They had a result on a night game. We weren't there ourselves but I guess a result is a result but again Savo knows what we're all about. Same goes for fat Pat of Chelsea. He's always been there for me whilst I've been in prison and knows what our crew are about as well. Time has taken its toll on our crew. The Old Bill and the CCTV have finally won. I also guess the area we're from ain't the best. The old Tiger Bay has mostly gone now and so have some of our mates, killed, imprisoned or been taken by drugs but the bond that we formed over the years is still there. We're still about but a lot less active and the police will never let us forget but swarm on us as soon as see us. Viking is still on a 10 year ban and myself a 6 year. So, thanks for the time lads.

Here's my opinion of the last 15 years and how I think other firms have done against us.

BORO are a very good crew. They stick together. Maybe haven't our numbers but can do the business and like I've said it's all about respect and we respect them.

SPURS excellent at their manor, numbers wise and quality but didn't show too much at ours. Can be dangerous on their day.

HULL never met really head on somehow the Old Bill have always won the day. A lot of times have been on a mid week game but on their day they hold their corner.

MAN UTD was the best mob I've seen at Cardiff for their cup final with Millwall. UTD another dangerous mob.

WOLVES I take my hat off to you all lads. Wolves who had a 500 strong mob out for us two seasons ago and can have it with anyone.

MILLWALL you all know their reputation and it's well deserved. They'll stand against anyone on their day.

THE ZULUS know us well and I think the feeling of respect is mutual, a strong outfit.

STOKE we took a naughty firm there a few years ago and tried our best to get at them. They are well respected in England and I guess by us. Just never really had a good battle with them but hats off to you lads, you can pull the numbers on the day.

BARNSLEY came to us and didn't come for show. They wanted it and not many teams do that in Cardiff.

BRISTOL CITY / SWANSEA have done nothing at Cardiff. They say a lot of things but when it comes down to it, the fact is they ain't got it and I doubt they ever will.

OURSELVES we can still muster big numbers but not always organised. When we are all together and I mean all our different firms including the Valley's we are unmovable on our day. I think it's all about who has the hardest lads and our front line are a pretty hard nut to crack. So although the scene is not the same anymore, there will always be a welcome in Cardiff especially if you bump into our crew.

Chapter 4
From Stamford Bridge to Ninian Park
Chelsea Pat

I first met Annis at Middlesbrough v Chelsea 1982/83 season. There had been running battles before the game in the town centre with Chelsea getting the upper hand. I had met Annis in the seats and had clocked his Cardiff City badge. I had always rated Cardiff back in the 70's when they had visited QPR and it was quite rare in those days to talk to someone from a rival mob. Anyway we clicked straight away and have become the best of friends ever since.

After the match about 50 Chelsea had cleared the Boro end until they had realised how many there was of Chelsea. They charged back and chased Chelsea onto the streets including my new found mate Annis. Another time, a Chelsea mob went around the Holt End and had a running battle with Villa all the way back to the station. After that game, I met Annis quite regularly up North and sometimes at the Bridge when his club Cardiff weren't playing. The best ones were Huddersfield away in the cup, Burnley away, Leeds away having a drink at Wakefield, Bolton and Grimsby. Annis was with me at all these games and they were proper legendary rows.

A funny one that's springs to mind is in the mid 80's. We ambushed Everton at High St Kensington. Annis had brought down Dexy and Zeddy, two Cardiff lads who were more than welcome by our mob. Annis had missed it but Dexy and Zeddy were there in a classic London underground ambush. "Fuck me," said Dexy, "I wish they had an underground system in Cardiff". We all fell about laughing.

Peterborough v Cardiff (late 80's)

Back in the mid 80's, I used to knock about with a mob of Northern Chelsea from Middlesbrough and Birmingham who were double game and over the years gained a big reputation at Chelsea. However fighting wasn't their only talent. These boys were experts in the art of breaking into fruit machines. This however was never my cup of tea. I never had the asshole for thieving and I'd rather fight ten geezers than steal a packet of polos.

Anyway a couple of mates of mine said they were going to Peterborough on a fruit machine tour and would I like to come. "Sure," I said on the understanding that I was going to stay out of the mischief. "No problem," they said, so off we went. We arrived in Peterborough and settled down in a pub/hotel opposite the station.

My two mates started to play the machine and, looking around, we were the only people in the bar besides a half sleeping barman.

I settled down with my pint and gazed out of the window. I remember looking up at the clock which said 11:00am above the station exit and then I was distracted by a huge mob walking out through the station exit. "Oi, who the fuck are these cunts," I shouted as I ran to my two mates by the fruit machine. Before we could react, the unknown mob swarmed into the pub and, from being empty, it was now packed with over 300 lads. Anyway, due to our casual dress (if I remember correctly, duffle coats were a fashion, the type with the wide wooden buttons), we were soon surround by about 10 lads. One of them was a big lump with red hair and he said "Heard of the Soul Crew Peterborough?" "Na mate, wrong mob, we're Chelsea," I said. "What are you lot doing down here?" said another Taffy. "We've come to see Annis, he's a mate of mine," I said. "Ok, I don't think he is here yet but you're more than welcome to come with us," said another lump. "Cheers mate." Thank fuck it was Cardiff who had walked into the pub and as I knew a few of them. If it had been anyone else, we could have been in trouble. Anyway as we were giving out the introductions, Brummie Andy said "As you're all here, you couldn't stand around this fruit machine while we break into it. We'll give you a drink." The Taffys didn't need asking twice. Crack! Bang! And the next thing the drinks were on us. Our new found Welsh friends invited us to go to the game with them and meet up with Annis. As we were leaving the pub, I had a tap on the shoulder. It was my old mate from Cardiff, Fisher. He was a mate of Nicky Parsons who was someone I knew at Chelsea. Fisher told me that him and Parsons had recently fallen out resulting in a fight. That was their business but it was good to see Fisher as he was a proper boy and as game as anyone.

When we arrived at the ground, all the Cardiff mob had seat tickets and, as we didn't, we told them we'd meet afterwards for drink. While we were stood there, another mob of about 60 Cardiff turned up led by my old mates, Zeddie and Dio. Zeddie used to come to Chelsea with me now and again and I would regard Zeddie as a good mate. He's now on the straight and narrow and you would never believe looking at him now how much he loved a footie tear up. He was a right chap in his day. Anyway we were persuaded into going into the ground with them and the first thing I noticed was that this little mob weren't as friendly as the Cardiff mob from the pub. "Argentina, Argentina" they chanted as a few glanced over at us while they were singing. This didn't go down well with my mates who said "Come on Pat, let's fuck off. I don't want to listen to this shit. We've just been in a war with Argentina." As we were discussing it, my mate Zeddie came over looking ashen-faced. He said "Pat, I'm so sorry, but you lot better leave because they are talking about serving you lot up." "It's ok Zeddie, we won't put it on you mate, we were leaving anyway."

As we were leaving, the main mouth piece of this group came out of the toilet and fucking withered as we all stared at him. I'm sure he pissed his jeans as he couldn't get back up into the terrace without walking through us. However, we're not liberty takers and just laughed at him as he ran past us and, do you know what? I've never seen him since.

Outside we walked around to the Peterborough end behind the opposite goal and, as you looked from the home end, Cardiff's main mob were up in the seats to our right, about 300 handed. The away end directly opposite had an open terrace on our right which contained about 50 Peterborough casuals who were plotted up next to the away end. We hung around to see what might happen. At the end of the game, Cardiff steamed out of the seats and charged straight across the pitch to the small mob of Peterborough facing them. Peterborough ran down to the wall and stood until the last few seconds before Cardiff climbed the wall. With that Peterborough turned and ran out of the back of the stand. Then the Cardiff mob turned their attention to us but luckily the Old Bill made a line in front of us. Cardiff then went on their usual rampage. On our way back to the station, we bumped into Fisher and the big red headed lad from the pub. They said they had seen Annis and that he'd come by car and he'd been looking for you Pat. When I told them what had happened in the away end, they went mental. "Who were they Pat ?, fucking point them out." "It doesn't matter, no-one got hurt so forget it," I said. "It does matter," said the red headed lad. "It does matter. Those bully cunts tried to take liberties with four blokes. Promise me Pat, if you see them, point them out." "Ok," I said but there was no way I was going to do that.

Anyway we reached the station without further incident and said goodbye to our newfound friends. On the way back to London we all laughed as we promised ourselves to make sure we checked the fixture list before any more unplanned weekends away.

Hayes v Cardiff (1990)

Ha, Ha. Let me tell you about Hayes Town FC from West London. If all the local football lads followed that team it would be like going to Millwall in the 70's at Cold Blow Lane. It seemed that West London were especially out that day. Some of the best quality boys from a dozen different mobs. You had lads from Chelsea, QPR, Arsenal, West Ham, Man Utd, Millwall, Brentford etc - all coming together when Hayes get a decent FA Cup draw.

Over the years, Hayes have slapped Swansea, Peterborough, took over Fulham and done Northampton away and as everyone knows, back in their day, Northampton at home were no mugs. Also they turned up at Ninian Park but as Lakey says in his 'The Soul Crew' book, there was no Cardiff mob out that day. Lakey also mentions that Hayes had a massive mob out because of the liberties Cardiff had taken at QPR during the previous season. No mate! As soon as Hayes drew Cardiff, about ten mobs around London woke up to the chance of a good punch up. It's a shame that they moved it from Hayes to Brentford because it would have been carnage.

Come the night of the game I was with about 25 QPR. There were Chelsea faces everywhere when we arrived in Brentford. When we all went into the first pub, a sea of ugly faces all faced our way and then slowly turned back to their beer when they realised we were Cockneys. Every pub was packed solid with chaps and my hand was getting sore from the amount of handshaking I was doing. I was seeing people who I had not seen for years.

Diary Of The Real Soul Crew

"Why is it that you get on with every cunt?" said an annoyed Gregor who was glaring at a load of Cockney reds (Man Utd) who were returning his stare with interest. "Now, now, Gregor. We're all Hayes tonight," I said with a grin.

On to the game. In the stadium, it turned out that Cardiff had a shit turnout with only a couple of hundred fans if that. It looked like we had come down from Shepherd's Bush for nothing. Me and my mate Smithy didn't go. We walked past the away end to see a young Cardiff lad being thrown out by the police. I called him over and at first he was understandably weary.

"Nah mate, we're sweet," said Smithy. "We just want to know if you have any boys down."

"Only about 20," he said.

"Is Annis there?" I asked.

"Yeah, he's inside"

"Fucking hell, I haven't seen him for about three years," I said.

"Tell him if you see him that I'll be looking for him."

With that we walked away as a nosey policeman came walking over. After the game about 300 - 400 lads gathered across the road from the away end. Apparently Cardiff had been cheeky in the ground so there was going to be no squeezes for them. The police did their best to break up everyone and move us on but, because it was dark and I don't think the Brentford police are too clued up for that sort of thing, we were all still there when Cardiff came out. The next thing I see was a group of about 25 lads with a few Old Bill protecting them come walking up the road. They might have well have painted them bright yellow as everyone moved towards them. Within minutes, there were 60 in front of them, 50 behind them and 200 odd walking beside them. They were 'dead men walking'. In the middle of it all, I heard a familiar voice screaming at the top of his voice, "Keep together, don't let them mingle in." Fuck me, it was my old mate Annis. I couldn't believe it. He was as white as a ghost but he was still barking orders to hold it together. I hadn't seen him for years and I was so pleased to see him that I bowled straight through the Old Bill right up to him, "Annis, my old mate, remember me?" I said. "Pat, you Chelsea bastard," as he hugged me. "What you doing here mate? This has turned into a nightmare for us," said Annis. I told him, "Just keep your head down. You've got no chance tonight. There's about 300 top boys from all over London looking to pay you back for 30 years of Welsh hospitality," I told him.

The next thing from behind I was grabbed out of the Cardiff escort by an angry Chelsea copper.

"What are you fucking doing, Pat?" growled the copper.

"I'm collecting my money," I said.

"What money?" said the copper.

"We had a bet that Cardiff would need an escort after the game. He lost," I said pointing at Annis.

"Get your fat arse over the road before I fill it with my boot, you cheeky cunt!!" roared the Old Bill.

I didn't need to be told twice. Anyway I was glad to see Annis and the boys Jonathan, Malo, Sandham, etc. as they managed to survive what was a dodgy night for them. Believe me, if it had been at Hayes FC, they wouldn't have been so lucky.

QPR v Cardiff

QPR drew Cardiff in the cup two years on the spin and there had been trouble at both games but the second one stood out. Before the game, it was unusually quiet with no Old Bill on the Uxbridge Road. I walked down with two of QPR's main boys, B & Gregor. We passed the police station and we were opposite the House of Pies chip shop. As I glanced over, a bus pulled up at the stop next to the chip shop. In front of us, there were four fellas who were all football chaps, two were eating chips and staring across the road at us. We clocked them looking at us and we all seemed to stop at the same time to stare at them.

"What are you looking at, you English cunts?" one said as he dropped his chips and bowled into the road. As we all looked at each other, the rest of them came over as well.

"Fuck this," said B. "What did you say, you fucking Cardiff cunt?" he asked. We flew off the pavement towards them.

"Come on then."

As we shaped up to our Welsh counter parts, the bus at the bus stop pulled off revealing about 40 of their mates, all stood there eating chips, oops!!!

"Come on you, Cockney cunts," went up the shout as Cardiff charged into the road.

"Baked potato" (see you later). Fuck me, I have never run so fast and, as people that know me will tell ya, I'm not built for speed. I turned into Lime Grove and I could still hear the roar behind us.

"Don't fucking leave me," I screamed at B and Gregors as they started pulling away from me. I could hear B laughing, "Keep up, you fat cunt. They're right behind ya." I somehow found a second wind.

I later found out they had given up chasing us virtually straight away but the other two kept me running as they thought I could do with the exercise. Fucking comedians!

After the game, QPR mobbed up at the Cunningham Pub. There were maybe 200 with hammers, bars and knives supplied by the local shops and pubs because people were sick of the Taffys - they had taken liberties once too often over the years. A couple of scouts plotted Bloemfontein Road and, as Cardiff turned towards Shepherd's Bush, they tried to bait them to walk the opposite way where QPR were waiting no more than 200 yards away. Cardiff never bit. I'm glad in a way because if they had of come down that road, there would have been a blood bath. It was pitch black, no Old Bill and with that amount of weapons, someone would have been killed without a doubt. Fair play to QPR, they later took over 100 to Paddington but the Old Bill stopped them on Praed Street. They were well up for it and respect should be given to them.

Cardiff v Bristol City, early 2000's

I hadn't been to Ninian Park since the legendary 3-3 draw game in which there was fighting all day long. Chelsea won the day off the pitch with our enormous numbers and maybe out of 6,000 fans, 3,500 were looking for trouble. Cardiff had a good go with at least a 1,000 lads but we had three times their numbers and, on the streets, they couldn't live with us. One thing that did piss us off was that Cardiff managed to hang on to that 'Fucking Bob Bank' again. It was the one end we regularly tried to take and were always fucked out of it. Hey ho, such is life.

The next time was a night game in the mid 80's during the police raids. Our firm was struggling badly after Hickey, Terry Last and all the rest had been pulled. Teams that you wouldn't dream of before started to turn up at Chelsea and take liberties. You knew things were bad when 40 Ipswich turned up and stood outside the Shed End as bold as brass at 2:00pm on a Saturday. Back to the night game in Wales. As usual, Cardiff had a huge reception committee outside the grandstand, maybe 500 odd. Chelsea had about 30 lads top whack and they were terrorised as they were put into the away end. One of the lads, Linky was nicked with a flare gun on his way into the ground. When he went back to Court in Cardiff the following week, he told the judge he had seen the flares in Italy so he thought it was legal to carry them. The judge fucking believed him. What a result. If that happened now, you'd get a 5 easy. Anyway, Linky's luck was about to change. Unknown to Linky, he was being watched by three Cardiff lads in the dock. As Linky reached the station, the three Taffys steamed into him. Linky managed to get onto the platform where luckily the London train was waiting. "You fucking Welsh mugs," said Linky as the train pulled off. To his horror, the Cardiff fans ran after the train and jumped on. Linky fled through the train pursued by the Taffys until he managed to lock himself in the toilet. The Cardiff lads kicked and punched the door all the way to Newport where they left the train. Poor old Linky. We laughed our heads off when he told us what had happened.

Anyway, back to the present. Annis had been on at me to come and visit a Cardiff game so it was in my mind to do it. I already knew loads of Cardiff boys, Mac, Big Sam, Christian, Little Pete, Steve D from when I go out to Thailand plus I knew loads more. Also a load of Cardiff were with Chelsea's firm against Arsenal at the Millennium Stadium cup final a few years before and they were all sound lads. The game at Cardiff that I went to was against Bristol City. At the time, the Bluebirds had just been taken over by Sam Hammam and the place was buzzing. I arrived on Friday night and I stayed in a hotel because Annis has loads of Alsatian dogs and I'm allergic to the fuckers. I met up with Pete, Christian and a few more and went on the piss with them. Apparently Bristol were bringing a big firm so it sounded like there were going to be fun and games.

On the day of the game, I woke up with a fucking horrible hangover and would have liked nothing more than to have stayed in my nice warm bed but there was a punch-up to be had so no laying in my pit today. At about 1:30pm, I followed the directions Annis had given me to the Exchange in Canton only to be met there by 200 grizzly's drinking out on the pavement and the pub was fucking jammed with about another 400 inside. They all seemed to stare at me as I approached. "Excuse me, sorry mate, excuse me," as I pushed my way through the bar to meet Simmo, Bowen, G and Lakey etc. who were all at the back of the pub. It was to be a great afternoon. I met loads of lovely people who would turn out to be friends forever.

Onto the game, everyone poured out from 3 pubs near one another at round 2:30pm. "Fuck me," I said to a Cardiff lad. "You must have a 1,000 lads here." He laughed. "Pat, this is nothing to what's waiting in the city centre." As we came around the corner, everyone charged up as they had heard that 200 Bristol were there but there were loads of Old Bill holding them. Bristol seemed well up for it as they pushed towards us only to be held by the riot Old Bill. Beyond them in the park, something was going on. A Cardiff lad put his arm out and pulled me up onto the wall and said "Pat, have a look at this." Fucking hell, there must have been at least another 1,000 Cardiff trying to attack Bristol from the other side on their escort. "That's the mob from the town," said the Cardiff lad as the Old Bill started to baton us up the road. Eventually we entered the ground and we sat in the upper Grandstand seats where I was joined by Annis.

The ground had changed since the last time I had been here. They had stuck a roof on the away end (Grange End) and some smart cunt had decided to share it with the home fans. It looked a lot like the old West Ham set up with the away fans pinned in the corner getting shit from the cunts next to you plus in the paddock down the side of you. Fucking marvellous. Whoever designed this ground (a throw back to the 70's) deserves a medal for hooliganism. The place was safer in the 80's and that's saying something.

Bristol had about 2,000 fans with maybe 200 lads pinned in the corner. Cardiff were all around them throwing missiles which were being flung between the mobs. You could actually pick out a Bristol face and shout at them because you were that close to them. You had to see it to believe it.

I sat there looking at the Canton Stand and Bob Bank and remembering the big fights we had with Cardiff over the years especially the big fight when we tried to get into the Bob bank at the back of the Canton Stand. I smiled to myself. "What's up Pat?" said Annis. "Just reminiscing," I said and carried on deep in thought. After the game which Cardiff lost (the team were still shit) then what I can only describe as the biggest mob I have seen since the early 80's gathered in the park. There was at least 2,000 boys, probably more. The police brought Bristol towards the exit and they gave a steam towards the street. This was a trigger that began a massive riot. Cardiff laid siege to the police lines for nearly an hour with every missile you can imagine and, in the commotion, I lost everyone so I popped into the Ninian Pub to see if I could find anyone. As soon as I reached the bar, I felt all eyes on me. "Where are you from mate?" said a big baldy lump. "London," I replied. "I'm a lad from Chelsea and a guest of Annis, Simmo etc. and I have seem to have lost them in the trouble." "You Chelsea, are you?" said another one. "Yeah." With that, they bought me a pint and for about 2 hours I had a great time with a bunch of Valleys and other lads from Port Talbot whilst going down memory lane. Top, top fellas.

Eventually I found my way back to the Exchange pub. "Where have you been?" asked Simmo. "In the Ninian," I replied. "Fucking hell, Pat. Be careful mate. You're lucky you weren't killed. Them Valleys can be really funny especially if you're English." "They were as good as gold, Bruv." Later on, I met Simmo's missus, the lovely Pam and Sian who remains a very good mate with her boyfriend Mike. As the night wore on, a big lump came up to me and for the first time all day, I felt a bit wary. "You're Chelsea," he growled. "Yeah, I am," I said. "What do you reckon of our mob then?" he snarled. "Mate, your 2,000 strong mob have just landed in the 2000's and you just smashed the Old Bill. Who's going to budge you lot?" With that, he broke into a smile. "You're fucking sound you," and he walked away. It was my first meeting with the legendary Viking. Later I was to meet his partner in crime, Jonathan and we all became firm friends. We still laugh about that first meeting now when we see each other. As I said, it was a blinding weekend and I have been back several times since with my mate from London, Gypsy Ben and other mates and have always been made welcome.

CCFC a top firm with top people.

100 fans in court after soccer clashes

SOME 100 soccer fans will appear in court today following clashes between rival supporters attending the Cardiff City - Chelsea game at Ninian Park on Saturday.

Police were called to scores of separate incidents inside and outside the football ground and disturbances occurred in Cardiff city centre before and after the game, which Chelsea won by two goals to one.

South Glamorgan ambulance service were called to 17 incidents involving soccer fans and about 20 people were treated in hospital for minor injuries.

One supporter had his jaw broken and police said a man would appear in court today in connection with the incident. Charges against the fans will include using threatening behaviour, carrying offensive weapons and assault.

The main trouble spots were public houses, and at one stage a police spokesman sai dthe situation was "chaotic."

At the Terminus public-house in St. Mary Street some 30 or 40 fans clashed and the landlord, Mr. Tony Cuddihy, said the cost of the damage was likely to run into hundreds of pounds.

At least 1,000 Chelsea fan travelled to Cardiff by train, most them on two soccer specials. Of t arrests about 50 were made by Tran port Police.

DAMAGE IN CITY AS FANS CLASH

FIGHTING broke out between rival Cardiff City and Chelsea fans this afternoon in the city centre and on the way to Ninian Park football ground.

The main trouble spots were public houses and Cardiff Police described the situation as "chaotic."

At the Terminus public house in St. Mary Street a large plate glass window was smashed, and there were reports of fighting outside The Albert public-house and in Ninian Park Road.

Mr. Tony Cuddihy, manager of the Terminus, said that between 30 and 40 Chelsea and Cardiff fans were involved in a disturbance at the public-house.

He said the window had been smashed by a stone throwing fan and glass in a door was broken by a beer glass.

Extra police were on duty for today's game and members of the Special Support Group were keeping rival fans apart at the ground.

A police spokesman in Cardiff said: "We have had reports of trouble through-out the city centre and on the way to the ground." He said 10 fans had been arrested by early this after-noon.

● The last time that Chelsea played at Cardiff at Ninian Park more than 100 fans from both sides were arrested.

Chapter 5
From Ely Trendies to Cardiff Soul Crew
Michael Dye, CCFC

Cardiff City to this day have had a massive mob and can call upon hundreds of lads when needed. Although football violence is a thing of the past (in the stadium anyway), it is not uncommon for violence to occur around city centres and pubs of every club to this day. Cardiff's Soul Crew was formed many years ago in the early eighties by a lad called Parsons but by 1984 he had been kicked out by one of the older lads. In the 83/84 season, me, Jammo and 'Rip' Rayer had travelled to the game at Leeds. We were young 15-16 year olds. We had boarded the 7:50am from Cardiff which arrived in Leeds at about 12:30pm. The drink was flowing and I think it was settling a lot of nerves. This was the Leeds Service Crew we were heading for who, at the time, had a huge reputation in the hooligan world. You could feel the tension among our ranks as if we were in awe of them. In reality, we were.

We passed on the train, Elland Road to our left and we all stood up to see an impressive stadium. We all thought that it would only be a short walk to the ground. How wrong we were. The train just kept on going. Someone shouted, "Fuck me, look how far we have to walk," in a nervous voice. We were entering unknown territory today. Last season, it was Bournemouth and Bury, this year it was Leeds and Chelsea. We finally came to a halt and piled off. We were dressed in all our finest clobber and it fucking pissed down all day. My Pringle jumper was soaked and Jammo's wedge haircut all wet and stringy. We left the station, all 250 of the Soul Crew and as we looked across the road with hardly any Old Bill around, we noticed Leeds had about 50 lads waiting. It could have been a great result for the young Soul Crew although we greatly outnumbered the Leeds Service Crew. The fun that day would have been running them which is a result in itself. At the time, Leeds, Chelsea, West Ham, Millwall and Man United were top of the yobs and we could have taken a great scalp. Someone amongst our ranks started chanting 'Cay-ardiff' and most others joined in. Then the Soul Crew chant went up. It was awesome. The real football lads in the know travelled by train, sat in the stands and didn't sing so how raw we were! Leeds fucked off sharp and our chanting alerted the Old Bill who surrounded us and stopped any possible action. Leeds actually called us the 'Welsh Male Voice Choir' for our efforts. We lost 2-0 and we had learnt a valuable lesson. From this day on I have never sung since!

I lived in Ely, an estate in Cardiff which was mostly council houses. Our area was lower Ely. We could pull together a real tight firm from around our patch and, when they got to know us, lads from Canton, Llanedeyrn, Splott and Whitchurch as well as most other areas of Cardiff would come and join us. Like I said earlier, we lived in lower Ely and we used to knock about by the local shops, especially one shop, called Maggie's Chip Shop. I believe it's now called 'Chippy on the Bridge'. It was situated right by a set of traffic lights opposite the Old White Lion pub. The front of this shop had three sections. Each one would step up about 4" to the entrance. We spent many an hour here and it would be the place to meet. It's also the place we first met the author of this book. We were eventually tagged as Millbank. For every person who remembers passing us at this point, I hope we never offended?

We travelled everywhere from 81/82 season. Me, Jammo, Rayer, Zub, CC, Zedy, Mosh and many more, too many to name them all. Thanks to you all for many great away days. I'm 41 now, with numerous Court convictions behind me for football related issues and in '87, I received a 9 month banning order - yes, 9 months, not prison. Just a £400 fine and the order. Most of my mates had convictions for disorder at football but before jail sentences were handed out as they are these days, banning orders and fines was the normal thing. Only my mate Baggars has done bird for his efforts.

I met Annis about the 84 season. Two of his best mates, Peter M and Little Collin, had by now started knocking around with us and they introduced us to him. I had heard stories about him regarding Bradford. After hearing his side, I don't doubt him. He did his best to get the pub full of Cardiff down to the station but it wasn't to be. We started travelling together. All young lads but with big hearts. The Ely Trendies as we were known also had a few punks amongst us. One went by the name of G.

We were at the heart of travelling. Some lads would wait at the station ready for the train but would not travel until we had turned up. We would always swell numbers by 20-30 and, due to the fact that not many travelled anyway, this was considered a large group. By '84, ourselves, Canton, Splott and the Docks would be in harmony. Travelling together, we looked good and had our fair encounters. Below are a few stories from our travels. Although not always violent, the laughs, running opposition fans and getting run ourselves were par for the course!

Man City '84

We took the train for this one. A big turnout of about 200, all dressed to the nines. Man City's firm in those days were called the Maine Line but we didn't give a fuck. We were going to Manc land. We downed some ale on the way up. I was a four pack man back then, no more or I'd be unstable on my feet!

Our train pulled in and we surged off. Hardly any Old Bill at the station platform. We went outside in search of the waiting Manc mob. We were not disappointed. Outside were maybe 50 Man City and also 2 double deckers to herd us to Maine Road. There were police vans, dog handlers and horseback riders. The Mancs didn't reckon on so many coming but the police had it sorted or had they? As the dibble forced most of our lot onto the buses, me, Jammo, CC, Peter M and a few others waited until the end and began baiting the Mancs. After about 5 minutes or so, we could see that about 30 of us couldn't get on the buses due to them being full. The buses were rocking back and forth by now. Anyone who has ever been upstairs on a double decker when it rocks with 80 idiots on board knows what I mean - Pepsi Max has nothing on that!

By now, all the Old Bill were busy trying to control the bus situation. This was our chance. We headed for the Mancs and fair play, they duly obliged. They were into us with punches and kicks being thrown from both sections. There was no standoffs. It all lasted only 60 seconds before the Old Bill were on top, man handling everybody. The fuckers had ripped buttons off of my brand new G2 shirt which I had bought from London only the week before. Never mind, that's life I suppose. I looked at it different than that though. I thought "Fuck, another £50 down the drain." The police had ordered another bus for us stragglers and within 10 minutes, it had arrived. We boarded with no problem but only after our day had been made. Man City brought a coach to us with their mob later that season. It was the first organised coach I had witnessed but the day went off without any trouble.

Exeter FA Cup '84

By the time this fixture had come about, we were travelling in massive numbers. Our train was full to the brim and when we arrived we piled off looking for a good pub or the opposition mob. This was one fixture where we learnt a valuable lesson about lesser opponents. We turned right after we left the station and marched on. After a while, our masses were splitting up (because of stragglers, etc.) Myself and Lucky Evans were up front, just looking for an ale house. Up in the distance we could see one, so we quickened our pace. Outside was a lad. I ran across the road and lashed out at him. He punched back and, being about six foot, well he could have been more like 7ft, he put me on my arse. With that, Kev was into him, punching out like an idiot. The lad was eventually overwhelmed by numbers and scurried off. What started as a 1 on 1 ended up more like Custer's last stand! Later that day at the match, we saw an old face in Alan Rawlings who had been stabbed in Blackpool by some Brummie Zulu Warriors whilst on a weekend break. When the match ended, we all ran onto the pitch. What I can remember most was about 15 or so City fans hanging from the goal post. My mate Rayer was hanging on and I thought I would join him. I don't know if it was my 8 stone weight or what but it seemed as soon as I jumped on, it broke, leaving our lot sprawled on the floor. Rayer was nicked for this and still blames me to this day!

On our walk back to the station, we yet again split up. While walking through town, one of my closest mates, Jammo, came out of Boots or somewhere with about 20 older heads shouting "Where the fuck have you been? We just had it in the shop!" They put up a good show and had stood their ground. Like I said earlier, never underestimate the smaller clubs. Some of them hate you and are out to prove a point.

Bolton Away, Part 1 '84

Myself, Jammo, Rayer and CC, all the usual characters from our estate plus we now had another part of Ely hanging about with us. Through high school we met Lucky Evans, Mogs and Tabby to name a few. We totalled about 12 in numbers and for this game it was train travel again. On leaving Bolton station, we turned right with no immediate pub in sight. A man of oriental appearance was passing by and we shouted "Where's the nearest pub mate?" He looked over and pointed "Just up there on the left." Right, we thought. With that, he quickened his pace and was off. As we reached the top of the road, maybe 40 or so Bolton lads appeared and were yelling "Come on, you Welsh cunts," and came towards us. Now these men must have been in their late 30's early 40's and we were only 17 maybe 18 years old. There was only 10 of us but we were fitter, quicker and 'Better Looking'. That was it. We were off. We went diving into shops and other establishments and out of the back doors and, luckily for us, they didn't pursue us for long. They were big ugly beer monsters with all the gear on. We ended up back in the station and by now the police had arrived to escort us to the ground. We felt braver now. The fuckers stoned our train home on the way back and everyone on the train hit the deck including ourselves and mothers with their kids.

Bolton Away, Part 2 '85

We ran a bus for this one to Manchester then the train into Bolton. This time we knew the set up. All the usual suspects turned up for this one plus other older Ely boys. A right motley crew this time. We arrived at Manchester and boarded the train. We headed to Bolton for noon and went straight for that same pub but this time it wasn't to be all one way. Bolton spotted us and out they came, maybe 70 of the fuckers. They didn't think 50 lads would be heading towards them but we fucking were. They shouted, "Come on" and we ran at them. This time it was their turn to scurry off. The few who did make a stance were punched and kicked until the police arrived to contain us. They put us in a pub but we had gained our revenge and enjoyed the rest of the day.

Chesterfield '85

This was yet another Friday night game and the 8 of us who travelled didn't expect any bother. This matched passed off without incident but all was not good. We left the ground after witnessing a rare away victory. Little Collin, 'Lucky' Evans, Moggsy, myself and a few others arrived at the station to head home. When I checked the timetable, it said we had 90 minutes or so to wait so we decided to head for a pub. After a couple of drinks, we left but didn't realise Little Collin was not with us - he must have gone to the toilet. As we waited in the concourse of the station, the sliding doors opened and in came about 25 drunken Chesterfield fans and about 10 from the rear entrance. We were trapped. The roar went up from Chesterfield and they were into us. Not much we could do really apart from fight back. I remember 'Lucky' and Moggsy being attacked first, then we were all punched and kicked. After this onslaught, they seemed to stand back and we thought here's our chance, let's get the fuck out of here! On exiting the station, we all drifted off in different directions with Chesterfield in hot pursuit. Hadn't the fuckers done enough to us already? I turned right on exiting the doors and headed for an old concrete building about 50 yards away. I reached this building and found there was an electric supply station over looking the motorway. I could also sense there were a few still chasing me. This building had a 2 foot wide path either side so I headed for the left side for no particular reason. As I reached the end, I came to a sudden halt as it overlooked the motorway. I bricked it! But looking to my right this path went right the way around and back out. Luckily for me, Chesterfield weren't clever enough to split up and go both directions but actually followed me around the one way! The drop overlooking the motorway was about 20 foot - god knows what would have happened if they had caught me. It's not something I like to think about or talk about since it happened. This trip has always haunted me knowing the fact it could have cost me my life. They followed me back to the station where a train guard had called the police. A few of our lot had already returned to the station and were advising the train guard who not to let in. On feeling safe once again, a sorry face turned up at the station doors with cuts and bruises to his face. It was none other than Little Collin who they had attacked some time earlier. Our train arrived and we all went home with our tails between our legs and not for the first time!

Tranmere '85

As either Liverpool or Everton play at home on the Saturday, Tranmere always play their games on a Friday night. About 20 of us travelled by train. Little Collin, Jerky, Rayer, myself and all the other usual suspects were on board.

There was no trouble before or during the match but after the game something occurred that was rather spooky. The Old Bill laid on meat wagons for us to get back to the station so we could catch our train. The 3 meat wagons travelled for about 10 minutes and dropped us off at a station which looked like a ghost town. It was very quiet with no other people waiting for a train. Later, we realised why there was no other passengers - it was closed! A few of us moved closer to the platform edge to listen for the hissing of the tracks when a train comes in. After about 10 minutes of waiting, we could see figures in the distance coming our way. This was Tranmere's lads. Little Collin noticed first. This was a definite set up. About 80 Tranmere came rushing down the steps and Little Collin headed straight for a wooden bench and started to dismantle it so we could use the pieces for our defence. We surged forward and to our dismay, they just flew into us. A few punches were exchanged and our weaponry thrown at them. Looking back, we should have held on to our weapons because, within seconds, we were overwhelmed and on our heels! We scurried off along the railway lines like rats into the night for what seemed like an age. Eventually, we reached an opening in the fence and all scuttled through. As we regrouped, we noticed we were in a very rough council estate and could see a pub up ahead. Now this pub looked rough but fuck it, we slammed the doors open and in we surged. The pub went quiet and everyone looked in our direction. Although there was no trouble in the pub, it was what lurked outside which was the problem! We used chairs and tables to block the doorway ready for the onslaught while the locals looked on in disbelief. We could hear Tranmere's lads outside, baying for our blood but before anything else could happen, we heard the sirens of the police. Was this a set up or our sanctuary? I'm pleased to say it was the latter as they escorted us to Lime street.

Diary Of The Real Soul Crew

Gloucester '86

One little trip away with Annis in early days was quite funny. Myself, Jerky, Chrissy Beer and Annis who drove, went to Gloucester for a friendly around the 1986 season. I was about 19 at the time and on parking the car we walked to the railway station to meet fellow City fans. Jerky decided he needed a shit and off he went. Me and Chrissy Beer decided to fool about so we went into the toilets to cause mischief. Jerky's cubicle was at the far end and all was quiet so we picked up a litter bin and threw it over the top of the door whilst Jerky was in full thrust. The bin disappeared and a scream was heard of "OUCH, YOU FUCKING CUNTS." In the melee, we hadn't noticed a train guard coming behind us. The noise the bin had made before landing on the lad shitting was fucking loud, imagine it hitting the walls and litter falling out. The guard shouted "Oi!" and went to ring the cops so we ran and yelled "Run" and Jerky entered the platform doing up his jeans, hotly perused by the train guard. We quickly fucking scarpered and went all different directions. My heart was racing and I lost all the others by entering a shop. I could hear sirens outside but they didn't catch any of us. This scarlet pimpernel was way too quick!

Bristol City '01

In 2001, this fixture brought together two real enemies. It was a night fixture and our train mob was huge. To put numbers to it, I couldn't. Baggers, Lucky Evans and myself travelled by car with Lucky driving. We never saw anything before the match as we had a drink right by the suspension bridge. After the match, we had gone what we thought was the right way but, to our dismay, it was leading us right into the Bristol fans. We decided for safety reasons to turn round and head back to the away end. You know, safety in numbers. As we walked towards the away end, we could see our lot coming up the road behind us, although not many. Then we heard a roar go up. It was Bristol's mob charging around a corner. They looked real angry and we were caught behind them. Cardiff at first retreated and Bristol were on top with only a few Cardiff standing and fighting back. A shout went up from Cardiff and they stopped and turned. By now, we were getting closer, fighting took place from one side of the road to the other and before long Bristol were on their toes, well, most of them anyway.

Myself, Lucky Evans and Baggers were amongst it now and we had no choice but to get stuck in. I remember all to well hitting a Bristol fan and him hitting me back and then both of us getting caught by more fans of both sides. This was his chance. I heard a spraying sound and the fucker had used pepper gas on me. I was bent over and it had gone dark and my eyes were stinging. Another punch landed on me and, as I looked up to fight back, I noticed it was a well known Cardiff fan who could look after himself. He noticed that it was me that he had hit and apologised a hundred times. By now the fight had stopped and the police had control. My face was stinging and very red. My main concern now was to get away before the police picked me up. Baggers and Lucky who were also slapped about, decided on getting me to a pub to clean up and make our way home.

As far back as I can remember, the two Bristol teams have always come out 2nd best when it comes to facing Cardiff. I feel that in recent months they have had a bit of revenge on us but with bullying tactics. For example, on March 4th 2008, (my birthday incidentally) Annis, Justin, Penny, Craig, Peter M's stepson, my lad and myself travelled to Crystal Palace. It was a Tuesday night match and there wasn't that many matches going on that night in London but one struck me straight away. Bristol City who were at the top at the time were playing at the Valley. We had a good drink on the way up and met up with Chelsea Pat and even bumped into 8 Olympiakos travellers on the tube getting ready for their match the following night with Chelsea. On arriving back at Paddington afterwards and with only minutes to get the last train home (11:30pm) we jogged to the train and just about made it. On board, it was full with the bully boys of Bristol City who had played Charlton. With our 6 and their 150 odd, we knew we were in for a rough ride home. They were in our faces all the way back giving Annis a right old time of it. If the Old Bill hadn't been on board, we would have been beaten and thrown off at Reading. We made it home unscathed although at Temple Mead where most of them left the train, we were told to keep our heads down as they were likely to put the windows through. They never did.

About six weeks later, we travelled to Burnley. Dan, James, my wife Nathalie and myself caught the 6:25am train out of Cardiff. Whilst at the station we noticed two young City fans so we asked if they would like to join us on the journey which they accepted. I now know these two lads as Dean and Pip who I have a lot of respect and time for and boy can they drink! Pip brought along 8 bottles of Foster's twist - he hated them! And on every swig he would say 'yuk'. We arrived in Burnley at 11:30am and consumed yet more ale before attending the game. We left with the score at 0-0 and headed for the station via the ale house when the police entered the pub and advised us to drink up and head to the station for our own safety. Dan and Jayo had stayed until the end of the match. We were supposed to meet them in the pub but as the police moved us on (we had already waited a while for them). At 5:30pm, we rang to tell them what platform we were on only to hear they were already on a train. I said "You can't be. Our train doesn't arrive until 17:45!" They then realised they were on the wrong train and heading for Bradford!

We boarded our train and had to change at Preston and Birmingham which took two hours. Our connecting train was the Leeds to Plymouth line. On checking the fixtures, I noticed that Bristol City were at Sheffield Utd. Funny thing, this train housed not only 100 Bristol supporters but our very own Dan and Jayo! Reunited!

As we had walked through the carriages, an oldish guy with a worzel accent made a suggestive remark to my wife and I heard this. I went over and had a few words with him and he eventually apologised. This was the calm before the storm. We found seats and were actually chatting to some Bristol fans about how they had got on etc. On arriving at Cheltenham, Pip said to me "Who the fuck are all them lads on the platform?" Problem was we had to change yet again here. I then noticed 60-70 lads who were also Bristol but must have caught the earlier train out of Sheffield. This was their mob. Stone Island United by the looks of it! They didn't seem bothered with us at first and don't think they noticed our crew (well there was only eight of us, two kids included and a lass). They were at the other end of the platform. As we stood on the platform waiting for the train, two of the Bristol scumbags who had got off next to us spat at my wife and I can tell you she wasn't best pleased. She gave them a mouthful and then I had yet more words! This frustrated the two lads and they shouted to all the other Bristol fans as if to say "Let's have 'em, it's fucking Cardiff". They didn't come up the platform straight away but as a train pulled in, about 40 of the twats came towards us. They surged forward and threw everything they could at us. The air was filled with flying bottles and beer cans. We were now dodging all this. The bottles smashed and bits of glass reigned supreme. We returned the favour with what beer we had (two cans I think!) If only Pip had had any of his Foster's twist left, I'm sure he would have launched them! This bought us all of about five seconds breathing space. We were all standing together and my words to everyone was "No-one fucking run, just stand our ground." Fair play to our lot. We didn't budge. They came closer giving it the "Come on, you Welsh cunts" but we were not going anywhere. If we had of run, they would have been in the driving seat with sheer numbers. They got right in our faces yet we still weren't moving, just stepping back a bit waiting for the onslaught. I had noticed by now that they were coming around the side of us but still they never attacked. With that, one of them became a bit brave and came charging in, smacking Pip to which Pip responded with a hell of a punch. They stood off again. The ones to the side of me were wary. They were giving it the large of "Come on then" but, being well out numbered, it wasn't clever for us to make the first move. By now, more of them had become involved. We still stood firm and, on another attack from Bristol, more punches were exchanged and our two new recruits Dean and Pip did us proud. There still wasn't a copper in sight. This could and should have been a walkover for them although, if the boot was on the other foot, we would never have attacked eight including a woman under any circumstances.

Further up the platform we could see the yellow jackets of the police. If I'm honest, it was a welcome sight. They moved the bully boys from Bristol onto their train and it pulled off. We then boarded our train and headed for home. After this episode, I have lost all respect for Bristol City. It must be true what Bristol Rovers say about them. Respect to Dean and Pip for helping out that night and well done to my son and wife. Looking back I wonder if this was some kind of revenge for all the years of beatings they have taken.

Battle at New Street, '02

One of my favourites was the scrapping and running of the Cockney Reds at New Street station. We had travelled by train to Northampton and found out that the game had been called off. So we decided to stop off in a pub. Anthony, Robbie, Morg, Justin, GV, Pernny, Lucky, Bags and a few more names were on this outing. At about 4:00pm we decided to make our way back to New Street as the Mancs would be coming through. We left the station to make our way to the Wetherspoons in town for a quick few and guessed on the Reds coming though about 7ish. We had a bit of banter with a gang of Asians at Brum who barged into us on purpose. One barged me so I turned and fronted him. We squared up and he went to headbutt me but I moved out of the way and Goughy was into him throwing numerous punches. Before we could do anything, it was all over with our lot actually saying pack it in they ain't worth it. Fair play to 'em, there was only about six of them. We had a few drinks before heading back to New Street. Our main group drank up and left but Justin and GV were lagging behind as we left the pub and were about five minutes behind us. Guess what? The Asians we'd come across earlier had mobbed up and waited for the main group to leave and they then attacked our two stragglers causing them cuts and bruises. But that is what it is all about.

On arriving at New Street, we went into the pub on the station and after about ten minutes, a policeman came in and closed the pub. He wanted us out of the way because the Cockney Reds were due in. We were not happy but felt that with no beer, there was no point in stopping. We headed for the platform and made our way down the stairs for the train. Lucky Evans was just being thrown off the chugger for smoking! The copper who was dealing with us pleaded to the guard to let us on but the guard was not having any of it. Myself and young Anthony who is a quality lad decided if Lucky Evans couldn't get on the train then none of us would and made our way back up the steps. On reaching the top, fuck me, the blue of Brum had turned to the red of Manchester. These were the shirters - where was the mob? With that, we saw their dressers. We were all pissed but ready, although a bit unstable. The Old Bill didn't know what to do. There was twenty of us, two cops and Man U's mob coming up the stairs. We surged forward to where their platform was and, as we approached, the local plod surrounded us pushing us all up against a wall. Normal people were getting out of the way but we surged again to break out of the police hold and tried to get into the Man U who by now were coming into view. As we got into a few of them, I went to lash out at one Manc and he raised his leg (as it was warm he had shorts on) and showed me his Cardiff City tattoo almost as if it was in his defence. I had to ask the question "Who the fuck DO you support?" to which I had no reply.

We let up a roar of "SOUL CREW, SOUL CREW" and barged through again but this time the truncheons were used to strike us and I remember crawling down on the floor with a couple of ours doing the same while the truncheons rained down on us. Fuck me, we had some bruises. While all this was going on, apparently the rest of Man U had heard the roar and ran back down the stairs. The dibble were very heavy handed mind and we did have three arrests for public disorder of which two received heavy fines for their troubles. I then stepped back on the train to head home. My phone was red hot with people ringing me, asking me what had happened. News spreads fast in the soccer world.

Plymouth '02

I organised my own coach for this one as was the norm for these days. This one was a Tuesday night game and Plymouth were game. After stopping off just outside Plymouth, we had a rendezvous with the local dibble who would then take all the coaches in together to avoid trouble. How wrong they were. We arrived third in

Diary Of The Real Soul Crew

line behind two supporter's coaches run by Vince Alm who does a tremendous job running these coaches. As we pulled near the car park at Home Park, the first coach stopped and so on across the road. The Plymouth firm were standing there egging on our supporters coaches. They never banked on us at the back. Robbie spotted this and the rear door opened and everyone piled off. Plymouth having roughly the same numbers soon had it on their toes, running to a nearby park. Cardiff pursued them. On reaching the park, they did make a stance against the eight Cardiff lads who had chased them the full distance. We were not stopping now and we were into 'em. Strange as it is, most of the Plymouth fans ran again but the ones who stood took a hiding. We thought that was it but as we approached the ground, they regrouped. We were now all in 2's and 3's. They punched every City fan they came across. Arrests were made but for some reason, they were all Cardiff. Myself and Lucky were nabbed and held until after the game. They then released us and we made it back to the coach for home. Two weeks later, a summons for Court was delivered. Fair play to Vince. He travelled down to the Court the second time as a witness along with my mate CC, Annis' brother-in-law Jamie and my solicitor Mojo. I received a not guilty which was only fair as I didn't do anything. Good on our justice system for that one. For everyone that was there that night, well played boys.

Brighton '04

Brighton was another tricky little trip especially on a Tuesday night. There was nine of us on a hired a mini bus. We set off about noon and arrived about four hours later. We found a pub just on the outskirts. Baggers, Zub, Lucky Evans, GV, myself and a few others got the drinks in. After a few hours, we left for the ground. We could see up ahead about 50 Cardiff being escorted to the ground by the police and about 20 Brighton giving them lip. We noticed this and sort of 'mingled' with the Brighton lads. At first, they were unaware of this. I noticed their main lad was a bit of a pie eater and we aptly named him 'Fatty'. Zub and myself stepped up right close and said to him "Here we are, big boy!" He was a bit stunned at this and we all carried on walking to the ground.

As we approached the ground, the main Cardiff lot turned right under escort and ourselves and Brighton went left. Fatty realised we were still amongst them and said "Come on, you Cardiff cunts." It needed a good right hand to sort him out! All his lot were shaping up ready for the fight. Fuck it, I thought and so did Zub as we both laid into him at the same time. With this, Brighton attacked and Lucky Baggers and GV fought back. It was sort of even numbers to start with but being so near to their end, they came from everywhere and soon had us backing off. This separated the two sets of supporters. We goaded them after it had settled down, saying "what the fucking hell was that!" and Fatty scurried off for a pie, also gaining a Lacoste watch which I lost in the fracas. But fair do's to Baggers, he claimed a Hugo Boss cap and said "Never mind, Dio, you can have this cap to replace your stolen watch" A £10 to replace my £100 watch. The thought was there, I guess!

Cardiff have never claimed to be No1 and truth be told, probably never will be but we give it our best shot and like anybody else, we can come out on top unlike the so called Jack Army who have never lost a battle, have they? My recollections on those bastards from down the road is we would overrun them every game and take over. I would actually say just like Chelsea did to us. We would terrorise them. A paragraph from their 'Book of Truths, The Jack Army', they always claimed that their fixture would always land on a Easter Sunday or when no trains ran; well, we normally played down their place on New Year's Day, no trains too but would always fill the away end and normally the side enclosure too. We can all remember when a Cardiff fan ran on the pitch at the Vetch and started to fuck a plastic swan which was sited on either penalty spot. Can anyone remember a Swansea fan running on to aid this poor Swan? No! These were the years when the Old Bill were not clued up but we always travelled.

One year in the late 80's, Annis hired a coach and 50 of us young 'uns went to Swansea Leisure Centre early and had a swim before the game. All paid I think! We went into the pool with our bundies and boxer shorts on. How the fuck we dried off, I will never know! We then walked along the Jacks' seafront and straight into their town centre. No Old Bill and no Jacks as usual in them days. By kick-off, our numbers had swelled to a few hundred and we were once again able to walk around with no Jack in sight. The Old Bill eventually rounded us up but where were you Jacks in the 80's? It started becoming a bore down in Gypo land. I noticed the Jacks did turn up in small numbers throughout the late 90's and when we've played them in the last few years but the police have always had a grip. Work it out for yourselves boys....

Summary

The Ely boys and myself plus all the many lads I have met over the years no longer take part in this long gone disorderly era. We have all moved on and attend most games but if a situation arises like the Bristol City at Cheltenham situation, you have to defend yourselves. I have been married for the past three years to Nathalie. I have four children (Becky, James, Chris and Jake) and two step children (Luke and Hollie) and I have realised that there is more to life than football violence. It's the 'fooligan' way of life.

I will finish with all the best to Cardiff City and by the time you read this, we hopefully would have won the cup! (We never)

Addicted to hooliganism

A former member of Carlisle's notorious Border City Firm (BCF) hooligan group, Charters eventually swore allegiance to their Cardiff City counterparts, known as the Soul Crew, whose name is tattooed on the back of his head.

Wednesday, 12 March 2008

A VETERAN Carlisle hooligan pleaded with magistrates to help him beat his life-long addiction of organised football violence.

News & Star

Scott Charters

Scott Charters, a self-confessed hooligan since the age of 14, was given his second football banning order for the latest in a long series of soccer related convictions.

The court order yesterday bans him from going to any professional soccer match in England or Wales for the next three years. It was imposed after police arrested Charters on Botchergate following Carlisle United's game with Doncaster Rovers on Saturday, February 23, magistrates heard.

Members are from all walks of life, he said, and they include lawyers and doctors. For many, hooliganism offers an adrenaline rush, combined with an enduring and tribal sense of belonging.

Charters explained: "As a kid, I'd watch Carlisle and go into the Warwick Road end at Brunton Park, and stand there next to the big lads, watching and listening to what they were getting up to. I felt I was part of something, and got a buzz from it all. I felt pride in what we did. It felt like people were looking up to us.

"I eventually got sent down for football related offences and moved on to the Cardiff Soul Crew after meeting friends in jail."

Contrary to the common view, he claimed, soccer hooligans live by an unwritten code that should protect genuine fans, known among hooligans as "scarves".

He said: "We don't go near normal fans. It's firm against firm . As soon as somebody is on the ground, that's usually it.

"Nine times out of ten, when somebody's on the ground they don't get stamped on."

He spoke of seeing hooligans suspend hostilities as women and children passed by.

He said most firms are on good terms when not in direct combat. He pointed out: "I was fighting the Red Army [associated with Manchester United], and I ended up pulling a lad's tongue out of this throat after he swallowed it, and I put him in the recovery position." He went on: "People often ask me why I've got involved?

"It's also an addiction."

Chapter 6
Barry Soul Crew Seasiders
Jeff Marsh, CCFC

I grew up on Barry Island which, at the time, was home to the Butlins Camp and a very busy fairground and docks. At age 15, I was a Skinhead. Myself and all the other boys from school used to hang around the promenade on weekends. On Bank Holidays, we would fight with Mods, Teds, Asians, Greasers or anyone who wanted to know. We used to have mass stone fights over the fence with English kids from the Thomas of Beckett Homes who used to stay in the Camp on what was known as 'The kids weeks'. These went on for a good few years and we used to go down on the railway bank and collect buckets of stones, hide them in the bushes in preparation for these battles. Many a kid suffered head injuries in these mass rock fights and the sight of some English twat being stretchered away covered in blood was always guaranteed to cheer us up.

We had some massive brawls with Mods who used to come from Cardiff, Bridgend, Ponty and the Valleys. Most Bank Holidays, it was like a scene from Quadrophenia as running battles took place on the beach or promenade. One time, when I was around 16 or 17, I was sitting on the beach wall with about five other Skinheads and some blonde kid on the beach below us walked up offering us out. He seemed to have about four or five others with him so I jumped down and said "Come on then, let's have you.". He starts shouting "Come on Cardiff" and all of a sudden there's about 30 of these bowl haircutted kids running at us from all different directions and a lot of them had umbrellas and were running at us using them like spears. Someone was shouting "Annis, here they are" as we legged it up the steps and away.

That was the first time I came across Annis. Not long after, I took my first trip to football. It was the terrifying outing to Millwall which I wrote about in my first book and, although I hated football, I was hooked on this new gang war that I had discovered. Now in those days (early 80's), Mods and Skins often used to clash on the terraces of Ninian Park but that was all about to change. As Skins and Mods realised that they were being singled out by the police for attention at matches while these bowl haircutted, ski jacket and trainer wearing Herbert's which, at the time, were known as 'Trendys' could get away with murder with their 'boy next door' appearance. Before long, all the Mods and Skins were dressing as Trendies and the 'Soul Crew' name started to be bandied about. Now instead of fighting each other, we were forming into one unit with a common enemy which were 'firms' from around the country. It was easy to sort out disputes between different groups just by saying things like "Don't fight each other, save it for the Jacks/Millwall/Chelsea/

Pompey" or whoever we were playing next.

I next met Annis when I climbed aboard one of his coaches. I can't remember where it was going. I think maybe Wrexham but we spoke about the incident on the beach and laughed about it as it didn't matter now. We were all top mates and that was how it was going to stay. After this, I became a fully fledged member of the 'Annis Travel Club' and we travelled all over the place together and in my opinion, if it wasn't for Annis and his organisational skills, Cardiff would never have gained the reputation they did back in those days. The team's performance was terrible. You always knew Cardiff were going to lose. We were stuck in the shit divisions. It was grim but we travelled everywhere. Rain or shine, we were on the terraces of shitty Northern teams, going on the other teams ends, confronting much larger mobs and taking liberties. None of it would have been possible without Annis. He used to drive down to us and all round the Valleys convincing people that Cardiff's honour was at stake. OK, he was making a few quid off the coaches but we didn't care. As long as we had a bit of fun and a day out.

With the Annis Travel Club, we used to go by coach, fleets of vans or by train using Family Railcards (One adult pays full fare then an army of 'kids' can go for £1 each) or Persil Vouchers to get there cheaply. We used to go into supermarkets with Stanley knives and cut the vouchers off the Persil boxes, walking away as powder poured out everywhere. We went on many adventures to places like Blackpool, Bolton, Stockport, Burnley, Tranmere. One trip that stands out was a shitty night match at Halifax when around thirty of us made the trip. Five or six of us went on their end but had to get out quickly as loads of Leeds skinheads came into the ground. In those days, you could walk all around the ground so we headed back to the Cardiff end. We noticed that they were mobbing up and moving over towards us so we decided the best form of defence was to attack. We ran onto the pitch and headed for them. Around the edge of the pitch at the Shay stadium was a speedway track so I grabbed a rock, jumped into the terracing on my own and launched it at them. Next thing, I'm being chased all around the ground by the Old Bill. They decked me and bundled me out and into a van. I'm sat in a cell thinking 'this is shit' and wondering how I'm going to get home in the morning when the police came back in and told me I was being released as Annis (who had split all his head open when there had been a crash as they had driven around the town, looking for Halifax lads) had made the coach driver drive the coach full of Cardiff to the police station. All the boys had refused to leave until they released me. The police had been so desperate to get rid of them, they agreed to bail me straight away. A top result and I won't ever forget it. This is how proper mates should be. Never leave anyone behind. I can remember Annis was concussed and covered in blood all the way home then ended up in hospital. Apparently, the kid driving the car had only passed his test a few days before and had driven from Cardiff to Halifax! I remember some drama on the way home after the boys stole some crates of pop from a chip shop and the Old Bill came on searching us all. We could have done without that. I went back up to Court and was slapped with a £60 fine. It cost me more than that to get up there. What a joke!

Another mad trip was Darlington where we left Cardiff at around 5:00am or

6:00am, travelled all the way up there and when we arrived the game was snowed off! We had 'Saint and Greavesy' laughing at us on the telly and about 18 hours on a coach to show for all our trouble. Mind you, we stopped off in Ashby-de-la-Zouch and had a mass snowball fight and raided a few shops so that made it a bit more fun. Everywhere we went, the towns would be wrecked, pubs and shops smashed, cars overturned and battered bodies everywhere. It was fucking brilliant. I used to carry a blade as a matter of course in those days, mostly for slashing seats on Blackpool trams, London Underground trains, etc and ended up doing two years in one of Her Majesty's hotels for stabbing two filthy Mancs. I do regret the whole knife business as now I feel only cowards use knives. At the time, a few of our lads had been slashed and we started carrying as a result and the whole thing escalated out of control for a while. I don't however regret my life as a hooligan. Those were the best years of my life. We were lucky enough to be there through the Glory Days of the 80's and I had a top time and met some top lads. People can slate Annis all they want but as far as I'm concerned, he is a top guy and he made the Soul Crew one of the best mobs around back in those days.

It makes me laugh when I hear about people saying 'The Hooligans have wrecked Cardiff and claiming they have supported the club for the last thirty years'. The fact is, in those grim days of the 80's, if it wasn't for the 'Hooligans', Cardiff would have had no following at all and I don't remember us having many scarfers back in those days. I'd say we had around 250 lads who all knew each other and knew we would back each other to the hilt. Those days have gone now and the police have definitely destroyed hooliganism. It could never have gone on forever because it became out of control and a lot of people were hurt back in those days. With banning orders, CCTV, surveillance and massive sentences for what, in reality, are minor public order offences, only an idiot would want to be a hooligan these days. The worst hooligans I've seen in recent years are the police who will batter anyone they want at football events with no fear of reprisals. If anyone wonders where the thugs are gone these days, they all joined the police!

Jeff Marsh, Author of Soul Crew Seasiders

Diary Of The Real Soul Crew

12 August 2001
Manchester United v Liverpool
Cardiff supporters returning from their league match against Wycombe found the Prince of Wales pub full of Manchester United fans, in town for the Charity Shield the next day.

Police kept the two groups apart with drawn batons and the hooligans fought running battles with police through the evening. 22 people were arrested, including two Cardiff youths aged just 11 and 13. One fan was slashed and a police officer suffered a broken arm.

There was further violence before the Charity Shield game the next day when eye-witnesses described how a 50-strong mob of Liverpool and Cardiff fans attacked Manchester followers in Wood Street.

21 August 2001
Millwall v Cardiff City
A potentially explosive mid-week fixture in the first round of the Worthington Cup. In the event only a few hundred Cardiff fans made the journey to London. Very few hooligans from Cardiff's "Soul Crew" went to the Den.

However, after the game, young Millwall fans ran riot in the streets around the ground. Cars and shops were smashed and bricks and bottles were thrown at police long into the night.

9 October 2001
Bristol City v Cardiff City
The Cardiff "Soul Crew" hooligans were escorted to the Coliseum pub in Redcliffe Road. From there they were taken to Ashton Gate. Small groups of Bristol City hooligans were in touch by mobile phone to their Cardiff counterparts.

They tried to attack the escort at Ashton Park but were held back by the police. After the game 40 or 50 Bristol hooligans attacked Cardiff fans as they left the ground. There was hand to hand fighting before police horses charged in.

29 December 2001
Cardiff City v Bristol City
The Bristol City hooligan group of around 300 was escorted from the Old Monk pub to the ground. On the way they were ambushed by Cardiff's "Soul Crew", at Grangetown Station. The police baton charged the Cardiff hooligans.

During the game coins, cans and bottles of urine were thrown. Innocent fans were terrified. Cardiff hooligans racially abused Bristol City fans and ripped up seats.

After the game, Bristol fans returning to their cars and coaches were pelted with stones. Cardiff hooligans then fought with police for up to an hour. A local photographer was beaten unconscious.

6 January 2002   **BBC NEWS**
Cardiff City v Leeds United
Around 200 Leeds hooligans travelled by coach to Hereford, where they boarded a train to Cardiff. They were escorted to the ground. A small group of Cardiff attempted to ambush them on Sloper Road, but were easily pushed back by the police.

Leeds hooligans racially abused Asian families on the way to the ground. Outside the ground the Leeds escort was pelted with missiles.

During the match missiles were thrown at Leeds fans, who returned many of them. At full time Cardiff fans invaded the pitch and were prevented from attacking the Leeds supporters by riot police and dogs.

26 February 2002
Huddersfield Town v Cardiff City
Four football fans were arrested even though the match was called off due to a waterlogged pitch. A large group of Cardiff hooligans in the Cherry Tree pub was surrounded by police. Officers from four different police forces escorted the Cardiff coaches down the M1, blocking off exits with motorcycle riders.

2 March 2002
Northampton Town v Cardiff City
There was a brawl involving more than 50 people at the Sixfields leisure complex in Weedon Road, shortly before the final whistle. Missiles were thrown and nearby drinkers were showered with glass as windows were smashed.

30 March 2002
Chesterfield v Cardiff City
Rival fans fought with each other both before and after the match. Missiles were thrown and the police came under attack as hooligans from both teams tried to get at each other. The trouble lasted well into the evening.

1 May 2002
Cardiff City v Stoke City
Five people were arrested as trouble erupted after Cardiff lost in the Division Two play-off match.

Around 600 Cardiff fans gathered outside their Ninian Park stadium after the match as 800 Stoke fans were leaving.

Three police officers needed hospital treatment following the disturbance while a number of others suffered minor injuries.

Officers using batons struggled to keep the two sets of fans apart as missiles - including stones, bottles and fence posts - were thrown from the Cardiff side.

28 April 2002
Stoke City v Cardiff City
After the notorious fixture between these clubs in April 2000, police mounted one of the largest operations in the history of the domestic game. Staffordshire police, a small force of just 2,000 officers, called on other forces to turn out a thousand officers on the day.

The game was stopped for 7 minutes as the police attempted to arrest Stoke hooligans in the ground. After the game police were pelted with stones. Cardiff owner Sam Hamamm had his car vandalised.

13 May 2002
Cardiff City v Swansea City
Rival fans threw bricks and bottles at each other after trouble flared at the end of the FAW Cup final at Ninian Park. Riot police and mounted officers were used to keep groups of fans apart.

Several supporters tore down dividing fences in a bid to get at each other but were eventually forced back to their coaches by police. One police officer was taken to hospital with a shoulder injury.

South Wales Police had arrested 34 people before the game in an operation aimed at preventing trouble.

Chapter 7
Little Collin's Story
Little Collin, CCFC

I've been there during the 70's and been in the thick of it during the 80's. I've fought alongside the Soul Crew and I would like to believe I was one of the original Ely Trendies and Soul Crew lads. I hardly go now and when I have it's a totally different scene. It's now well and truly over. Those who know me, know that I don't give a fuck about a kicking. I've been stabbed, slashed and three or four times hospitalised and most of the incidents are actually away from football. I've been beaten up many times at football but I've given as good as I got and what brings a smile to me is when you're well outnumbered. Annis asked me if I would tell some tales so I'm going to tell you about two incidents at football that come to mind. I was more than happy to help Annis as we go way back and have been good mates at football and outside football for as long as I can remember.

The Ointment, Bradford.

Well, a lot has been said about Bradford and I'm sure Annis in his next book will tell you all about his own experiences regarding Bradford and tell you it in full but here's what happened to me. I was 18 years old when we played Bradford away and I will never forget the Bradford fight in the 1982/83 season. Being out numbered is a big buzz to me as is when the odds are stacked against you. You know who your real mates are and you can always sit back afterwards and have a laugh about it.

We boarded the train at Cardiff Central. Eight lads and one girl but I knew to be honest that the only one I could rely on was Worzel. Yes we knew there would probably be some kind of reception waiting for us. In those days, virtually every team in the country made a show. The journey was a seven hour long boring journey. I did expect more than eight lads to go but there you go. I thought "this should be fun". Eventually we arrived at Bradford interchange. We left the train and there were no reception for us on the platform. You could feel that everyone started to feel relaxed. We went down these escalators and as we reached the ground level I noticed a few lads at the bottom; I'd say about six lads. I thought these were their 'spotters'. Little did we know there were much more than six. From out of nowhere, a mob of about sixty Ointment appeared. Most of the lads with me were edgy as if to say, what the fuck we going to do? Worzel and I just carried on walking to the exit where they were crowded. I knew I was going to get a kicking but that's life. If you don't want to know, don't go! I think Bradford were disappointed

61

with our turnout and then they just suddenly came into us shouting "Ointment, Ointment." Worzel and myself were suddenly fighting everyone. I hit as many as I could but the amount of punches that rained down on me sent me and a few others flying back. I then noticed Worzel seemed to be getting a worse hammering than me so I went back and tried to help him. I would never leave a mate. They seemed to stop for a couple of seconds and we regrouped by the bottom of the escalators. They came at us again and our lot did have brollies and were whacking them back as Worzel and I tried to punch them back. Eventually we were forced back up the escalators to the platform. I don't know why but Bradford just seemed to disappear. Yes they had a result in their eyes but if they were so good, why were we not that battered? I actually felt more knackered and exhausted than battered and I was glad that I could finally recharge myself ready for whatever happened next. The Old Bill finally appeared.

At the ground I met my old mates, Annis and Mannings. They said they had heard there had been trouble but everyone knows what I'm like. I laughed as I told them the story. I have met some of the Ointment on a few occasions for a drink but not on a football day and to be honest we laughed about that day. They didn't stop buying me drinks and always say they had respect for me. We also met about 15 years ago at Valley Parade against the City and I think we showed them how it should be done.

Two Stanley's too many

A day at a football match is something you look forward to. You may wonder because you never know what is going to happen. I will give you an example. It was the mid 80's, a Friday night kick-off at Tranmere which is on the outskirts of Liverpool. About 15 of us left Cardiff train station at 10:30am Friday morning and made our way to the game. On the train, we drank a few cans and played a couple of games of cards. Eventually we arrived at Liverpool Lime Street at about 3:00pm. That gave us four and a half hours of drinking time. We caught a local train to Tranmere and settled in a pub near the ground. Anyway kick-off was drawing near so a few of us left the pub and went outside the ground to see what was going on. Nothing was happening so we went into the ground. First half of the game was a bit boring and when half-time came, myself and two mates decided to get a coffee and something to eat. Well, while we were queuing up, a few Tranmere lads started mouthing off and trying to wind us up. I did get a bit annoyed and said "Look, if you want to have a go, we'll play along." In the end, we exchanged a few words and went back to watch the second half. So we watched the rest of the game and when the final whistle went, we all left the ground and made our way to the train station. The Old Bill stopped us and told us they would take us to the train station. So they dropped us off at a station called Rock Ferry. It seemed a bit out of the way and deserted. Hanging around on the platform, waiting for the train, one of the lads went for a walk. He came back saying that a mob was coming into the station.

This is how it went. There were about forty of them and only about 15 of us so the numbers were against us to start with. Then, when they came closer, I could see that some of them were tooled up with knives. I knew this was a bit dodgy and pulled out my Stanley, thinking this is it. I looked around and some of our lads had started off down the track to get away. Things were going quicker than I thought. The next thing I knew there were only four of us left. This one lad of ours was trying to break up a bench so I went over and broke it up with him. There I was, a length of wood in one hand and a Stanley in the other. The next thing, there they were right in front of me and all my mates had run. I was on my own again thinking "how am I going to get away?" I put the Stanley back in my pocket and started to swing the length of wood around. I noticed they were backing off. So I had an escape plan only if it worked. This is it. I swung the wood one last time and threw it towards them and then turned and ran. I ran as quick as possible but inside me this was hurting me. I wasn't prepared to be sliced into mince meat. I would stand against fists or one Stanley but not half a dozen Stanleys. As I was running, I tripped over the railway line and twisted my knee. I thought "fucking hell, I'm in trouble now." I managed to get up and made my way to the fence. I don't know how I did it but I climbed over it. On the other side of the fence was a housing estate, I looked behind. Fuck me, they've gone! Thank fuck for that. Around the corner was a pub and all the lads were sat inside. I went into the pub and sat there talking about what had just happened. Looking back on it now, I sit and chuckle to myself. How did I survive? I guess it was just meant to be. I will say this, it's a fucking rough place Tranmere and you need a better mob than we did that night.

I am 44 years old now and in my opinion those were the best days. To this day Annis & Mannings remain my good friends and since that day we have been side by side on many occasions, I would trust them two with my life.

Diary Of The Real Soul Crew

Soccer violence mars Sheffield United Cardiff match

Sep 21 2003

Police said violence between groups of rival football hooligans at yesterday's Sheffiled United-Cardiff City match was the worst they had seen in many years. More than 150 extra officers were drafted in to police the Division One football fixture at Sheffield's Bramhall Lane ground. But trouble flared between fans both before and after the match, resulting in six men being injured and a further six being arrested. Police wearing protective equipment, mounted officers and a police helicopter were brought in after intelligence revealed that a group of Cardiff fans planned to arrive in Sheffield early in order to confront local hooligans. The 3pm match kick-off was delayed by 10 minutes while the visiting fans were escorted through the city from railway and coach stations. Problems occurred inside the stadium after the game, which finished 5-3 to Sheffield Utd, with coin throwing and abuse between rival fans. Police outside the ground used batons to keep opposing fans apart when the trouble escalated and Cardiff fans began to attack officers. A South Yorkshire Police spokesperson said: "Some Cardiff fans also turned on police officers in a number of violent incidents. "It was the worst we've seen in many years." Superintendent Martin Hemmingway added: "The enjoyment of a superb game of football by many decent fans was marred by the appalling behaviour of a minority of people who were clearly intent on causing trouble from the outset." Five Cardiff supporters and one Sheffield fan were arrested - two of the Cardiff fans were charged with affray, one with threatening behaviour and two with disorderly conduct. The Sheffield supporter was charged with threatening behaviour. Two police officers and three Cardiff fans sustained minor injuries in the disturbance and one Cardiff supporter attended the Northern General Hospital, where he was given treatment for a head injury.

■ 'PANDEMONIUM' Police confront fans outside the ground at Saturday's away game at Sheffield.

'DON'T BLAM

City fans fire back at police accusations

CARDIFF City fans have hit back at accusations from Sheffield police that they caused the "worst violence in many years" on Saturday.

Trouble flared before and after the Bluebirds' away fixture at Bramall Lane and mounted police wearing protective gear had to keep rival fans apart.

Six arrests – five Cardiff supporters and a Sheffield fan – were made. More are expected after South Yorkshire Police study CCTV, camera and helicopter camera footage.

Cardiff fans laid the blame for the trouble at the door of the police.

Valley Rams spokesman Gwyn Davies said: "The police started a full charge the length of a street when we were going back to the buses.

"Police horses were running through the crowds and men were being attacked in front of their children. It was pandemonium. Fans from our coaches were taken to hospital, one with a broken jaw, one with a broken ankle."

And Cardiff City Supporters' Club spokesman Vince Alm said: "Police control was amateurish. Our police force in South Wales is fantastic and I suppose we expect the same

high standards from others, but this was horrendous."

But South Yorkshire Police Chief Inspector Jim Haylett said fans on both sides – not officers – were to blame.

"The police will never start trouble but we have to respond to the intelligence we've got," he said.

"There were hundreds of people on both sides of the fence intent on committing

whole scale violence.

"You cannot solely blame Cardiff or Sheffield. This was co-ordinated football hooliganism where both sides were culpable."

Superintendent Martin Hemmingway said: "The level of violence towards police officers by Cardiff hooligans was extremely high. It was the worst we have seen in Sheffield for many years."

64

Chapter 8
The Cream of Devon
Con, CCFC

I could talk about my experiences at notorious grounds such as Stamford Bridge, The Den, Upton Park, Ayresome Park, St Andrews or Elland Road but I can hear people laughing when I make the confession that the scariest ground that I have ever had the misfortune to visit is St James' Park, Exeter. I have been there on four occasions to watch Cardiff City play Exeter City. When people mention Exeter, beautiful images of this leafy town full of character and ancient history are conjured up in most people's minds. Unfortunately I am going to shatter that illusion. Images of unhinged fighting, broken bones and no-holds-barred thuggery collide inside my mind's eye.

November 16th 1985 - FA Cup 1st Round:
Exeter City 2 Cardiff City 1 (Nigel Stevenson)

In 1985, you didn't support Cardiff City for the joys on offer on the pitch. They were dark days for the club struggling on the verge of footballing infinity. On May 11th 1985, we had been relegated from the old second to the third division after losing 2-1 to Wimbledon at Plough Lane. The date lived long in my memory as it was the same day as the fire at Bradford (more of which later). These were bleak times with a clueless manager, Alan Durban, at the helm. We really did have the worst football team in history.

My first taste of Devon 'hospitality' was a first round FA Cup tie. The Grecians had been promoted from the old fourth division to the third but as favourites we were still expected to win easily. In those days, the FA Cup was still a massive draw and most of Cardiff's major hooligans had made the journey to Devon. The trip had attracted a large crowd of eager City faces who had expected to see us progress against the lowly opposition into the next round of the FA Cup. I was only 16 years old, green to the gills but up for whatever was on offer. At the time, I was on a YTS at a government organisation and in truth, I also felt like I was on a YTS with the Soul Crew. I headed down to the South West with a large group of Grangetown casuals including Mallo and Coxy – we were the youngest boys when we started on the scene in 1983. We reckoned it was the mighty Cardiff on the pitch against the minnows of Exeter and the mighty Soul Crew off it. There was to be no giant-killing on or off the pitch – or so we thought.

As youngsters, we were too young to be served in pubs so had to content ourselves with the alcoholic joys on offer at the local Tesco. We watched on as all the older lads filled their gullets in Exeter's finest watering holes. For those who don't know, Exeter is a picturesque market town with leafy vistas popping up behind the many historic Tudor buildings. If you want tranquillity and serenity you picked the right place - except when Cardiff City come to town, of course. As we walked, cans in hand, the idyllic scene was shattered by what resembled a wild west brawl. I saw a guy in a Rangers ski hat (contrary to popular belief a lot of Cardiff fans in those days harboured loyalist sympathies). This was Jammo - a terrace legend who is worthy of a separate weighty tome - who was having to fight off three or four guys on his own. There was also Mark from Pontypridd, a granite built British Army boxing champ and a Chelsea fan who was having chunks of his hair pulled out by half a dozen guys. Mark was one of only a few Valley boys who were members of the Soul Crew at the time. It was predominantly a Cardiff, Barry and Port Talbot affair. There were literally hundreds of people fighting. This was way out of our league as innocent 16 year old Soul Crew youth trainees.

One of the boys, Maratzi, who was in the notorious B Troop from Llanrumney (a predecessor to the Soul Crew), had to be carried into a shop with a suspected broken leg, only for Exeter's Sly Crew to go in and give him another leathering before the ambulance arrived. Quite ironically, it was in a shoe store that he received this violent kicking. This ruck was so large and had spilled out so widely and wildly that the police were hard pressed to know where to begin to break it up. It had gone on for half hour at least but it seemed like an eternity. Despite their lowly reputation both on and off the pitch, Exeter gave as good as they got. There was sporadic fighting all the way on the long walk from the town centre to St James' Park - a mile or two at least. This was a taste of things to come. If we thought it was going to get better as the afternoon progressed we were wrong. The scenes unfolding were foreign to us. We were the mighty Cardiff City. It should be a stroll in the park on and off the pitch against lowly Exeter. Shouldn't it?

On the pitch we weren't faring much better, going down 2-1 to a team fired up by the volatile crowd. The game itself will live long in the memory for three incidents. A last minute penalty to Exeter being stopped as Cardiff fans invaded the pitch, the goal posts being broken in the ensuing ruckus and Cardiff City manager Alan Durban being attacked by his own fans incensed by what they saw as a gutless capitulation. Make no mistake this was a full scale football riot.

After the match, the assembled City hordes were gamely escorted from St James' Park to Exeter Central. As rioting was breaking out all around, the police were trying to manage the unmanageable, quell the unquellable and had to contend with not only physical exertions but were having their ear turned too by a large blonde-haired bloke and one of the poshest City hooligans I had ever met. Simon Williams, who was to become a director at the club, was unconcerned with the raw sights, smells and sounds around him but more concerned with retrieving his multi-coloured, country gent umbrella he had mislaid in the melee. All we could hear him repeating ad infinitum to any copper that would listen was, "I say, have you seen a multi-coloured umbrella? I appear to have dropped it somewhere round here." It was as if Lord Charles had taken a wrong turn into the marching hordes of Babylon.

It's funny what you remember, but as an eyes-wide-open 16 year old who had happened upon his first football riot, that stuck in my mind and gave us all a laugh – to break up the palpable tension - as we trekked our way battered and bruised to the station.

September 20ᵗʰ 1986 - Division Four: Exeter City 0-0 Cardiff City

This season signalled a new low in the history of the football club. It was the first time we had ever been relegated to the old fourth division. Durban had been served his P45 in favour of fiery Scotsman Frankie Burrows, a no nonsense ex-Swindon player who was a member of their famous 1969 team that beat Arsenal 3-1 at Wembley. Famous bedfellows that season were Wolves who had plummeted from the old first division to the fourth. Another big fish in a small pond. Revenge was high on the agenda after the battle of St James' Park the previous season. Two Transit vans full of Cardiff's finest which included Annis, Dexy, Martyn Davies, Dixie, Dexy, Rich E and a group of well up for it Barry boys. Also flying down to Devon in the back of the van was Boozer, a diehard Millwall fan who, despite being from Cardiff, had a body which was a human gallery of Millwall tattoos. Despite being a skinhead and thereby tarred with the racist brush, he famously launched an assault on an NF march in Cardiff. While his principles were still firmly in place, dispelling the lazy myth that all skinheads and football fans are fascists, he was still a headcase.

Once again the weather was warm, the scenery was stunning and as we weaved our way down the M5 after making an obligatory stop off in Taunton for a few Scrumpy Jacks, a few of the lads flung the doors open and hung their legs out of the bus. A risky manoeuvre as one wrong move would have sent us bouncing down the motorway on our arses – easy road kill for a passing truck! But when you're young and seemingly invincible, you don't measure risks to life or limbs. On arriving in Exeter, thoughts of the previous season's events got the adrenaline pumping, mixed in with the west country's finest cider. The sun was beating a path from the sky as we parked up next to the town's towering cathedral. Pretty apt for the sinners stepping out of the two battle buses. A huge police presence ensured that any pre-match rucks were kept to a minimum.

On entering the ground, it was completely different. Half a dozen of Cardiff's foremost fruitcakes decided to try and take the home end. Obviously they hadn't been to Exeter the year before. At the front of the charge were Neath Punk (another one who could have a book penned in his honour) and Fulman (probably one of the hardest guys ever to grace the Ninian Park terraces – an absolute monster). Despite putting up a gallant battle, they were overrun. If Rourke's Drift had been transplanted to a leafy Devon town, it wouldn't have been too dissimilar to the scene unfolding before our eyes. Neath Punk (playing the Michael 'Bromhead' Caine role) bore the brunt of his gallant efforts in the face of overwhelming odds. He 'escaped' with a fractured cheekbone and several other broken bones. If there was a VC for attempting to take liberties, he'd have been awarded it. Anyway he was used to living on the frontline, having a home just a few miles from Swansea!

The proceedings took another bizarre twist when City fans attempted to set fire to bushes towards the back of the away terrace. Thankfully, a raging fire didn't take hold, just a few random flames. This was mightily prescient given the next day's headlines would be full of stories of an arson attempt further north. That day Leeds United played Bradford City at the Odsal Stadium which is an old rugby league ground. It was a Bradford home game as their own ground, Valley Parade, was being rebuilt after the horrific fire that tore through it on May 11th 1985. Leeds fans set fire to a chip van and caused chaos at the Odsal. Luckily no-one was seriously injured and thankfully a fire didn't take hold at St James' Park. What did take hold was a lot of fighting at the end of the game with the Devon constabulary. I saw someone, who is now a sergeant in the South Wales police force, kick a copper and whose photo adorned the next day's Mail on Sunday and South Wales Echo. The Mail reporter Peter Walker, the ex-Glamorgan and England cricketer, famously described Cardiff City fans as terrace guerrilla warfare specialists. It may have been intended as an insult but, to most of City's battle hardened masses, they wore it as a badge of honour.

Talking of taking liberties, one ex-famous Soul Crew member used to 'violate' Peter Walker's daughter on a regular basis much to the outrage of daddy!

After a few minor skirmishes, we made it back to the transit in one piece. It was such a beautiful sunny day and after all the events on and off the pitch we decided to stop off again in Taunton on the way back for a few more ciders. Dexy, who was one of the first of a number of Soul crew members to be charged with rioting at a Cardiff v Swansea the following year (August 1997), nearly had the life knocked out of him at the pub in Taunton. He'd taken it upon himself to write CCFC in a newly laid concrete floor that had taken workmen all day to lay under the sweltering sun, only to see their hard work be spoilt. He was lucky to escape as the incensed Navvies fronted up but a bit of quick thinking thankfully defused the potentially volatile situation.

As an aside, the return game at Ninian Park on March 31st 1987 was famous for Exeter bringing the combined total of one away fan to Cardiff. Were they scared? Probably but fair play to the guy, he stood there defiantly facing a barrage of abuse from the City ranks with his Exeter City flag draped over a Grange End barrier. As you can imagine, chants of 'Is that all you take away?' reverberated around the ground all afternoon.

April 2nd 1988 - Division Four:
Exeter City 0-2 Cardiff City (Kevin Bartlett 2)

Our second season in the basement division but we were now going up finishing second only to Wolves after famously beating them at Molineux 4-1 on February 6th 1988. That season, we were taking huge numbers to every away game, a sizeable number of whom weren't there just for the on-pitch entertainment. Our now annual party at Exeter was guaranteed. A large crowd of us once again stopped off at Taunton where we grouped up before heading off to our favourite Devon town. The trip was memorable for a fight breaking out between two Cardiff fans. At the time, outsiders weren't always welcome by certain members of the Soul Crew. Mallo took exception to Matt - a half-American, Leeds-supporting fan from Cheltenham who now resides in the States. We met Matt on various travels around the UK following our respective clubs and he became something of a name when he jettisoned Leeds to become a fully paid up City fan. He even decided to move to Cardiff to declare his love for the Bluebirds' cause. All hell broke loose as a lasting animosity between the two spilled over in the pub. A lot of the Soul Crew saw it as bullying by Mallo, picking on anyone younger than himself.

The welcome was equally as hostile when reached Devon. We were attacked from Exeter station all the way to the ground. Fair play to the Sly Crew they were nothing but consistent. To underline their cheek, one guy walked towards me, went to shake my hand, head-butted me and ran off. We were in a small group and had to battle our way to the ground. It was astonishing.

On arriving at St James' Park, we managed to get into the home end. Out of an act of bravado and possibly sheer stupidity, we then found ourselves fighting our way out of their end as Rourke's Drift 2 took hold. All the sensible people were put on the football special from Exeter St James' station back to Exeter St David's. However around 20 of us had decided to walk back to Exeter Central instead of travelling on the football special train. At that age, most us were neither sensible nor fully realising just what we were letting ourselves in for. What we were was bang up for a ruck although, if we fully realised what awaited us a few hundred yards away, even youthful bravado and heavy-duty testosterone may have given way to common sense.

It was as we reached the cathedral (in our youthfully misguided eyes, some sort of eternal battle between good and evil scenario) and when we rounded a corner, we were confronted by a huge mob of 250 Exeter baying for our blood. I was shaking like a leaf when they started to quicken their pace from a walk into a run, their faces full of anger and striding with a common purpose. It was then that I heard Jammo utter the words that would go down in Soul Crew folklore - "Come on Cardiff, this is where we make a name for ourselves." I cannot describe the feeling of sheer terror as the Exeter horde tore towards us. Incredibly, as we faced up, it was as if the reputation of Cardiff and the fact that we stood firm rooted to the spot, had the effect of putting doubt in their minds. They couldn't quite believe, we had faced up to them. To be honest, neither could we. Seeing this show of defiance, Exeter thought twice, turned on their heels and ran. It was a retreat of biblical proportions in the shadow of the cathedral. Call it divine intervention but how we survived to tell that particular story, I'll never know.

The Footnote: August 12th 2000 - Division 3:
Exeter City 1-2 Cardiff City (Paul Brayson, Josh Low)

It would be twelve years before I headed back to St James Park. On my return the landscape both on and off the pitch couldn't have been more different. This was the very first match at the beginning of the Sam Hammam era. The day we played Exeter, on the opening day of the new 2000-2001 football season, the atmosphere around St James' Park resembled a carnival. Finally a man with money and lots of it had come riding to Cardiff City's rescue. Or that's what we thought at the time. Nevertheless, what we saw in a place where I had seen hooliganism at its very worst, was a party atmosphere where the promise of good times to lie ahead were the perfect antidote to the edgy, foreboding place that was travelling away with Cardiff City in the 80's.

Cardiff City football club had reached a new chapter in its life and, just as the club had moved on, so had I.

Chapter 9
Gregors QPR
Mark Gregory

I have supported QPR from the early 70's. I'm 47 years old now and I've seen it all through the years. It was really nice of Annis to ask me to go down Memory Lane about Cardiff and QPR over the years. I have a big respect for Annis as a mate. We go back a long way, way back to the 80's and I have also a lot of respect for Cardiff as a mob. When I was very young in the early 70's, Cardiff always had a good reputation for coming to QPR and causing murder. My first encounter was when we were playing them in a night game and all the older firm told me "Gregs, don't worry you'll see them in the Loft tonight". Fuck me, that was a buzz to be with the older firm as I was a youngster waiting for the row to happen.

The Loft used to have a big middle entrance. Everyone used to stand on the right hand side of this entrance. All the older guys stood at the top of the stairs looking down at the turnstiles and watching to see if any mob tried to sneak in. As we were looking down the stairs from our left, we heard a massive roar from the T bar entrance. "CAAYARRDDIFF". With that everyone ran up to the back of the Loft so they couldn't get behind us and take our end. I was rooted to the spot watching all the gorillas as I was only 11. They were going toe to toe in the middle of the Loft. I did think then of getting involved until this fucking monster with a beard ran past me screaming "Come on you English bastards" and head butted a Rangers fan. It was the first time I saw a full on fight at QPR of that type and I was hooked. The Old Bill must have had a timeout that day because you couldn't dream of that nowadays.

Getting back to the row, QPR had the higher ground and forced Cardiff down the front. The Old Bill then took them out and marched them onto the pitch at the away end. You could hear from the away end "Cardiff agro, Cardiff agro" and from the QPR end "You'll never take the Loft". After that, at the end of the game, hundreds and hundreds fought with bottles, bricks and anything you could pick up from the ground. It went off via the away coach park to the dog track at White City Station, up to the green at Shepherd's Bush. It made Roma v Lazio look like a slight disagreement. Being so young, I skipped all the way home and couldn't wait to tell my school mates and recruit a teeny bopper mob to ambush the Welsh cunts next year.

Over the years I came into my own and became a well respected face at QPR and also a hated figure with some rival mobs and a target. I don't regret that as I have always put myself at the front. Being so small, I made up for it with bottle, a little bit of front and sometimes a big mouth! Sometimes being so small makes you a bigger target than if you were 7ft tall and my big mouth made things worse. With my cockney wit, I used to love mugging off the other mob. Being that most of these firms were caveman, I became public enemy No1, i.e. every firm that came to QPR the first thing they would say was 'Where's Gregors?' or 'I'm going to kill that cunt Gregors'. They are still saying it to the present day. Don't get me wrong. It's a pain in the arse when firms and the Old Bill make a B- line for me but it goes with the territory. QPR have a naughty firm that can match anyone on their day especially equal numbers. Some of our top boys are quality as lots of the mobs that took us lightly found out the hard way especially if they bumped into the C mob or the Northholt mob or 'my little firm' who were from the Notting Hill area and Ladbroke Grove. We used to do our own thing and you wouldn't want to meet us in a dark side street.

My Chelsea mate Pat reminded me of a night game in the late eighties against Cardiff in the old Littlewoods cup. At the time, we used to meet in the Bushrangers opposite Gold Hawk Road station. I talked Pat into going to Paddington to meet Cardiff off the train and to tell them not to get off at the Bush but to stay on for one stop and get off at Gold Hawk Road where we could play with them. Pat didn't fancy it because Cardiff fans were a bit barmy at the time and, if you tried to organise something with them, they would be quite happy to put you in hospital just because of your accent. Somehow I talked him into it. When we reached Paddington, I was beginning to think that Pat was right. There were about 500 monsters on the train and as they stepped onto the concourse, it was like an invasion of an army screaming abuse at anything that wasn't Welsh. Pat said "I fucking told you, Gregors. You can't talk to them. They'll kill you as soon as look at you." "Fuck that. Watch me," I said as I bounced into a group of about 20 of them. I told them I was QPR and told them what to do and they said they would do it. As I walked back, Pat's mouth was wide open. It was so open you could have put a football in it. "It's called bollocks, Pat," I said as I smiled and walked past him. "Well if you're a black cat, you little cunt, some of your lives have just fucked off," said Pat.

Anyway back to the Bushranger. QPR were about 100 handed waiting with no Old Bill. The game was a 7:45pm kick-off. It was now 7:30pm and everyone said they ain't coming so this whole mob left and walked to the ground without seeing any Cardiff fans. However I was on a band at the time so I was stood with fat Pat and his postman mate Steve outside the Whitehart pub opposite the police station and 100 yards from Shepherd's Bush Station. Pat's mate, Steve the postman, had just bought a massive pizza from Dominos across the road and was offering it to me and Pat. Pat was on a diet at the time (again) so he refused it but you could see he was gagging for it. Anyway, as I shared the pizza, a huge mob walked out of Shepherd's Bush station. When I say 'walked out', that's putting it mildly. They charged down the road and battered anyone who looked like they could throw a right hander. They reached a point opposite from us and turned down the side street next to the police station. I thought, I'm not having that. Pat second guessed me and said, "Don't you fucking dare, Gregor." Too late. I'd followed up behind them and said "Oi" and with that they all stopped and turned around. I said, "What time do you call this? Where were you at Gold Hawk Road?" There was a spilt second silence then they turned as one and charged. Pat's mate Steve had a big slice of pizza in his mouth at the time. That went west. Fat Pat broke the 100m record for an 18+ stone geezer and me, well I'm Gregor, so they lost me in the confusion. Sometimes, it pays to be lucky and small. After the game, there were more scuffles but nothing major. It's a shame the meet didn't happen before the game it would have been special.

Back in early 2000 and we hadn't played Cardiff for a while but we heard they were coming massive to QPR as usual. It was a night game again and this brought out our biggest turnout for a few years. We heard that Cardiff were massive in Hammersmith (early doors) and they were also firm handed in the Walkabout pub but later, as the day wore on, QPR, had an early meet at the British Queen on Uxbridge Road. A couple of nosey youth had scouted Hammersmith and said Cardiff were huge and that it should be good later. Late afternoon, me and my mate Sean went for a stroll but at the same time had to be careful as some Cardiff would beat me like a Swansea fan if they recognised me.

As bad luck would have it, I had a call from my girlfriend that she had been called into work so I had to go and take care of my boy who was only 6. I was gutted as I knew tonight would be special. I just went and picked up my boy and then myself and Sean headed down the Uxbridge Road towards the Prince. My mate Sean was dressed like an advert for Burberry and as we were opposite the White Hart Lane pub, five lumps appeared out of nowhere and fronted us. "Come on boys. We're Cardiff." I thought 'shit', what about my boy! I'll never forget the cunt. He had a white Timberland Cap and Jacket and was raging drunk. He turned to Sean and said, "You look like a boy. Come on, Sambo." As my mate is half caste, this didn't go down well. "Come on, we're Valleys." My mate lost it so I tried to get between them and said, "Leave it out mate, there's only two of us and a kid." Luckily, the prick's mate pulled him away.

We had gone about 50 yards when the same cunt came running up behind us and started again. I turned to Sean and said, "All yours mate." Fair play to Sean; he said, "No Gregor, what about your kid?, we've got all night for these mugs." I was fucking fuming. I couldn't believe that anyone could front us with a little kid. What a fucking liberty. "Forget about it," said Sean as we continued walking down Uxbridge Road. Something made me look around and I saw the little nob we had just had shit with but now he was joined with about 30 or more of his mates and was now marching quickly to catch us up. I then heard those immortal words, "I'm sure that's fucking Gregor." To make it worse, I had looked around as the geezer said it so they must have thought, "Bingo." Just as I was thinking we're fucked, my mobile went. Apparently QPR's mob were rioting with the Old Bill and about 300 of our lot were just up the road in front of us. The caller said it was really bad with flares, gas and all sorts of lovely stuff. I thought the best thing to do was to walk towards the riot and draw these Cardiff into QPR's spider web and then serve the cunts up.

As we got closer you could see something was going on up ahead but unbelievably the mob behind us still hadn't sussed it. We could now see the British Queen and the Old Bill were in Roman Army battle squares trying to contain the riot. The

Cardiff behind had now sussed it and said, "Fuck that," and started to walk back. One of them walked over to me and said "I know your big mouth don't I." I replied, "I'm Gregor." With that, he jumped back like I had rabies. I clocked some QPR lads who were nearby and said, "Come on, they're here," but they didn't fancy it. Luckily for me, about 10 of our main lot had slipped through the Old Bill and came over to me. After I had told them about the liberty that had been taken, they were raging, "Come on, let's get the cunts."

About 10, and it was a naughty 10 trust me, followed up behind that Cardiff group as they turned into Bloemfontein Road. A mate took my son to one side and said, "Payback time, Gregor." We roared up, Cardiff turned and faced us, bouncing up and down. Then one of then shouted, "They've got fucking blades." With that, they started to back peddle. As we pursued them, they made a stand next to a rubbish skip. Here we go, I thought. Just as it looked like it was going to go mental, they all turned and ran. I soon realised why as hundreds of QPR came running up the road behind us. The Cardiff boys ran to the junction of Bloemfontein Road where it turns towards the stadium at South Africa Road. There, a huge Cardiff mob had joined them on the corner. 'Armageddon' here we come I thought as hundreds of lads flew into each other all across the street. The Old Bill lost control and, to be honest, nobody budged. In the end, however we started to back Cardiff up because of our huge and bigger numbers. We claimed that row on points.

Everyone was being dispersed and as I was banned, I couldn't go in. I stood opposite the ground. Behind me, towards White City Station, a huge roar went up as about 400 Cardiff shirts came running down the South Africa Road, steamed across the road and attacked the Springbok pub which was full of QPR shirts. A huge shirt v shirt battle took place before my eyes. I was laughing my head off as I'd never seen this for years. The Old Bill gradually got between the two sides and pushed the Cardiff shirts towards the ground. In amongst them, I noticed a few dressers. As I was looking at them, one threw a punch and knocked out a QPR div who was minding his own business. My big mouth opened as usual, "Oi, ya doughnut, why you hitting clowns." A war of words took place and I was suddenly surrounded. I thought 'oops, oh shit'. "You look familiar," said the Cardiff lad who threw the knockout punch. Luckily for me, a QPR spotter stepped between us and said, "What are you doing Gregor?" "Fuck all, I know them" I replied. Phew!

The Cardiff barmys were now passing by us singing 'Wales, Wales', only to be joined by a the mob of QPR barmys singing 'England, England'. It took about 2 seconds for the third riot of the day to kick-off. There must have been a 1,000 barmys and boys and normal fans going at it hammer and tong. The Old Bill completely lost it again and chaos reigned. A big gap opened next to us and a big taffy who was a ringer for Annis wearing a Burberry shirt bounced into no-man's land offering everyone out. "Oi mate," I said, "bounce 20 yards down the road where there is no Old Bill." With that he said, "What do you mean, boyo. I've bounced 200 miles from Cardiff to get here." I had to laugh. It's not like me to be lost for words, nice one mate as I laughed, 1-0 to Cardiff.

While the game was on I went back to my mate's house who was looking after my son. He said he would keep him for a few hours until after the game so I could go back for round 2. When I reached the ground, the Old Bill who had had a bad night all round, decided to let everyone out together. "Hello," I thought. We just started to get together when a wicked 40 v 40 row broke out. Everyone was taking lumps out of each other and one Cardiff geezer, wearing a woolly hat, was double game flying into everyone. He looked like he had snorted a kilo of Charlie in one line.

Just my luck, he then came at me. I ducked down and threw an upper cut. Fuck me, he was out before he hit the floor. One of my mates laughed and said, "You win, Gregor. What do you want, a coconut or goldfish?" It all soon died down and I went back home where I had a phone call that a van load of Taffys had chased three QPR boys. Unlucky for the Taffys, the QPR made it to a naughty pub where some of our top boys were drinking. Fair play to Cardiff, they jumped out their van, 15 handed, and squared up but they couldn't have been in a worse place or be caught by nastier people. It kicked off and a few stood for a short while before they ran and left the van. One Cardiff guy, probably the driver, stood and, along with another four who were also caught, took a terrible beating. It's every chap's nightmare to be caught like that but when you put yourself on offer, these things happen. It's just a shame that when it goes Pete Tong, it's always the game lads that get caught. Afterwards on the internet, some Cardiff cyber warriors had said QPR had taken liberties with the mob in the van and were out of order. Just remember boys who started it. Cardiff had chased QPR but came unstuck. Sometimes, shit happens if you play our game. You have to learn to live with it.

In the 2006/7 season we played Cardiff and, as usual, we were looking forward to it. It was at the start of the season, even better.

We have a tasty youth mob who, for the last few years, have been on the phone to Cardiff youth to sort something out but for one reason or another, nothing has ever come of it. Me personally, I have nothing but respect for QPR youth. They have proved themselves again and again over the last few years and have some right game cunts among them. It's good to know that when me and the older main firm knock it on the head, QPR will still be a mob to be respected.

Before the game, we had a solid turn out at the British Queen and were about a 100 handed. The Old Bill have since wised up and blocked the road on the corner of Uxbridge Road and Bloemfontein Road before a game - it only took 30 years for the cunts to suss that one out. The first bit of action came about 1 o'clock when they marched Cardiff barmys down from the Walkabout pub. There was maybe 1,500 of them and, as usual, you would have trouble telling the difference between divs and mob as the shits were growling at bystanders and offering everyone out who looked like a QPR fan.

I had already plotted up on the Uxbridge Road with some of my mates. I knew this wasn't their main firm who hadn't arrived yet. About 5 minutes later, another escort came down and this one was surrounded by riot Old Bill. "Here we go," I said to a mate. As they approached, all you could see was 200 bald, 40-50 year old honey monsters marching down the road. The nearest thing that could describe it would be the baldys gang out of the 70's film The Wanderers. Fuck me, they didn't half look the part. When they were level with us, the Old Bill clocked me and ran over and surrounded me. Obviously, all the Cardiff looked over and one said, "That's Gregor." I thought 'Oh Bollocks' as the whole mob pushed towards me, shouting insults and threats. I said to the Old Bill, "You caused this, you better make sure they don't break." Cardiff, all of a sudden, stopped worrying about me and charged up the road, only to be beaten back by riot Old Bill. Apparently QPR had come running down from The British Queen and, on seeing the Cardiff escort, started throwing bottles, bricks, etc. The Old Bill got between the two mobs and started to push Cardiff up Bloemfontein Road towards the ground. My new ban was in force and I wasn't allowed to walk Bloemfontein Road. Instead, I stood on the corner watching the Soul Crew getting marched to the stadium. One of them was a massive cunt, who I can only describe as Bluto who was the bearded villain who was Popeye's enemy in the 70's cartoon, managed to slip the Old Bill and bounced over. "We've got a massive mob here today boyo. You've got no chance." As usual, my mouth goes into full speech, "Yeah mate, you've got a good mob but we've got a brilliant mob. If you get to this point after the game, don't turn towards the station. Turn right towards our pub then we'll see who's the governors".

With that he looked at me kind of funny. "Don't I know you from somewhere." Then you could see it dawned on him. "You're fucking Gregors." I kept quiet as I took a few steps back. Fuck me, this cunt had no neck. "Yeah, I'm Gregors," I said. He then said, "I've been waiting 6 years to get my hands on you. I really fancy my chances on you," said Bluto. With that, I just started laughing. It was lucky one of the Old Bill had started to take an interest. Well Bluto, I'm sorry I ain't got no spinach so that's out the window. Then to top it all, he said in a right valley accent, "Jog on, Gregor." I thought I would split my sides laughing as I walked away but to be honest I was happy the big ape didn't get his hands on me.

After I left the area, a sniper firm of Cardiff came along later and attacked the Adelaide pub which is opposite the British Queen. There was a few chaps in there at the time including one of our main boys and his 15 year old son who they happened to front first. Bad move. The fights spilled out of the Adelaide and drew the attention of some of our boys who were banned and were drinking in the British Queen. The Cardiff mob were hit from both sides and received a good slapping. Apparently there was a German with them who was quite game. Some of our lot thought it was Ronald from Cologne but that was shit. I knew he was with Chelsea Pat in the stadium along with some of Pat's Kiwi mates from Belushis pub up on the Green. They were just here to watch the game. Obviously the German was guesting with a mob of Cardiff that day. I'm sure he'll think twice about coming back to West London after his stay in Hammersmith hospital!

After the game QPR were 200 handed and had a fucking wicked mob. We came down the back streets onto Gold Hawk road. Someone in front shouted 'Cardiff are up ahead'. With that, we charged down the Gold Hawk Road. Imagine the buzz. No Old Bill, your mobs at full strength and about to clash with a respected foe. As we approached Gold Hawk Road station, we saw no Cardiff - just fucking Old Bill trying to block the road off to Shepherd's Bush. Shit, fucking great. We cut down Shepherd's Bush market towards Shepherd's Bush station. Bad fucking move. As we reached the top of the market, 200 riot Old Bill in full gear just charged us. They went berserk. Heads were busted left and right. God knows how many went to hospital. As usual you couldn't see any of the police numbers so I suppose, as normal, the best firm in the country won the day again. Unfortunately for us football hooligans, the best firm always wears riot gear!

Later on this season, QPR were at Palace and Cardiff were at Charlton. We were very active this season so it didn't take a professional to figure out we might cross paths. We had gone to Palace and to be honest it was shit. A small mob of our youth thought they would have a look at Paddington to see if Cardiff are still about. Bad move. When they left the station, they were surrounded by about 20 Cardiff Grizzlies who, for whatever reason, didn't go to the game. All they kept saying to them was, "Where's Gregors. If you see him, tell the little cunt, he's dead etc, etc." One of our youth, God bless him said, "Fuck you. If you got something to say to Gregor, tell him yourself." Luckily these Cardiff were all right and gave our little young mob a bit of a squeeze!

The next time I saw the Rangers youngster, I told him it was really nice of him to stand up for me but he shouldn't have put himself on offer. A few hours later, three of our boys who are known to like a beer had decided to follow the QPR youth to Paddington to be nosey. As they were on Paddington station concourse, a black homeless nutcase approached them on the ponce for beer money. As the QPR boys were pissed, they gave him some money and started having a laugh with him. Out of nowhere, boom, they were surrounded by about 20 Cardiff dressers who fronted them saying, "Who are you lot?" "We're QPR and we're here for you Welsh cunts," said one of the QPR fellas. Before anyone could react, the mad black homeless guy has bounced into the middle and started to do Kung Foo moves. He said to the Taffys, "You fuck with my mates, you fuck with me. Come on, I'll fight all of you." With the shock of it and I don't blame them Cardiff backed off trying to work out how to deal with this head case. Whilst they were getting their heads around it, thank fuck for our lot who would have taken a pasting, the Old Bill stepped in. My QPR mates said they never found out that mad geezer's name but if he reads this book, he has free beer waiting for him in the British Queen next season.

Police shocked by QPR soccer thugs

'A small group of perfectly peaceful Cardiff fans were walking past the British Queen pub when virtually all the QPR fans inside rushed out and seriously, savagely attacked police officers and opposing fans. It was completely unprovoked' - police chief

POLICE horses were punched, officers were pelted with missiles and a man was stabbed in one of the worst scenes of football hooliganism the borough has seen in years.

Some 62 people, a mix of QPR and Cardiff fans, were arrested on Friday night – the majority outside the Loftus Road ground following clashes with police and opposing fans. More than half of these had been charged and appeared in court by Thursday.

The authorities knew it had the potential of being a volatile match and around 400 police officers were drafted in to control fans – normally it would be 100.

However, even the borough's top police officer, Ch Supt Anthony Wills, was flabbergasted at the violence towards opposing fans and police.

"The behaviour of a minority of both Cardiff and QPR fans was simply appalling. What it showed to me was the ferocity still present within certain groups of football fans and their willingness to attack anyone and anything," he said.

Before the 7.45pm kick-off, groups of unruly mobs of QPR and Cardiff fans threw missiles at police.

"A small group of perfectly peaceful Cardiff fans were walking past the British Queen pub when virtually all the QPR fans inside rushed out and seriously, savagely attacked police officers and opposing fans with bottles, bricks and fireworks. It was completely unprovoked," Ch Supt Wills explained.

He said that QPR had a small minority of troublesome fans and around 150 were involved in violence that night.

A QPR fan, who took his 14-year-old son to the match, said he was astounded by the violent scenes.

"It was like World War III," he said. "I couldn't believe it. QPR fans were fighting police as they tried to get to Cardiff fans. Fireworks, rockets, bricks, and bottles were thrown at police. I saw three to four distress flares fired in quick succession. They had come armed to cause trouble."

The 42-year-old father-of-three said it was doubtful he would allow his son to go to another match.

Mike Hartwell, QPR spokesman, told the Gazette it would have been irresponsible to have put a warning in the programme although they had insisted on tickets being bought in advance.

He stressed the stabbing of a 23-year-old caterer, inside the ground, was not serious and that he was treated by medical staff at the scene.

Mr Hartwell said there was very little trouble inside the stadium and that only a handful of fans had been arrested there. However, he admitted the stabbing and other acts of hooliganism were regrettable and that they would be working with police to see if lessons could be learnt.

Chapter 10
We Gave It Our Best Shot
Viking (Cardiff Docks), CCFC

I was born in Cardiff Docks which is a close knit community where everyone knows everyone and you look out for each other. I have known Annis way back since the early 80's and we've had a good friendship ever since. I started going down to Ninian Park in the 70's. I was a fan for many years but the atmosphere during those years would soon draw you in and nearly everyone was a lad. They were either fighting or talking about it. During the early 80's when I was going around with all the lads, the Docks were always fighting the Ely Trendys outside of football and I was always trying to keep the peace. I felt like piggy in the middle. In time, the football pulled us all together and we started hanging around Brownhill's which was a pub in Cardiff City Centre owned by Annis.

The first time the hooligan side of the football became serious was when us Docks lads formed our own firm called 'The Dirty 30'. We were still part of the Soul Crew at the football matches but, outside football every weekend night, we would be battling with the doormen of the nightclubs and any outside gang that came into the city centre and tried to give it the big 'un. Gangs from Birmingham and Bristol over the years have come down and tried to think they could walk over our town. They were dealt with and never came back again. Some of the main lads of The Dirty 30 was Jonathan, Pepper, Rusty, Princy, Jellyhead, Big Foot, Bigger, Weller, Porta, Jaja, Farrah, Derek, Starship, Brummie, Toddy and a few more. In those days, we were like brothers. We stuck together. Everyone knew they could never run otherwise it would have been dealt with back home.

I have a lot of respect for teams like Bradford, Newport, Barnsley, Boro and Hull as they have come to Cardiff and really wanted it. They have gone as far as to bring the battle to us where most teams don't even turn up or, if they do, they make sure they are in an escort (Tottenham, they just came to make a show of it and never once tried to break the escort).

You'll all probably laugh at who I'm going to mention as one of the best tear ups I've ever had. Remember, I've fought Millwall, Cockney Reds, Boro and many other top firms so I was surprised as anyone when it happened in May '93 in the town centre of Doncaster. We had just won the third division championship at Scunthorpe. The Dirty 30 had taken a transit with 15 of our naughtiest lads. Nothing happened in Scunthorpe. We just took the piss so, on the way home, we decided to stop off in a sleepy town called Doncaster or so we thought. We stopped off in a bar and we were soon on the piss celebrating City's promotion. An hour or so later, we were told there was another pub with Cardiff in down the road.

Diary Of The Real Soul Crew

It was the PVM (Good lads from Port Talbot). So we all decided we would take a walk and go and join them. I could see a few of them standing outside a pub across the road. As I was walking over, a lad of about 19 years old approached me and said "Donny wants it." "You what? Donny wants it?" I said, "Go and get Donny, I'll have it with him now." Then the rest of the lads burst out laughing and said "Donny's their firm." Then suddenly there they were. I couldn't fucking believe it. A mob of 150 easily including townies, every doorman in the town, football lads and who ever else wanted a fight was there.

I said to everyone, "Just shut it and walk towards them and as we get closer, just steam the fuckers." My heart was going. There was no more than 30 of us including the PVM. We were out of our heads. As we got closer, one of their lads came from nowhere and sparked a PVM lad out and that was it, every fucker was fighting. It was right on top from the beginning but we kept as a unit and we managed to spilt them right down the middle. As we were doing this, some of our lads were getting clucked including myself. We were up for this and, the more I could see some of our lads being hurt, the more I wanted to go for them and the more psyched up we were getting. We had now split them and managed to back one section of them off. Fuck me, to this day I will never forget the battle as it didn't seem to matter how many punches you threw, they just kept coming at us more and more of them.

The Old Bill arrived and they just came wading into us, whacking us with their truncheons. We couldn't believe it. The rest of the police were just shouting at Doncaster to back off while we were getting slaughtered and they were hitting us like fuck. They then marched us to the vans. The only thing the Old Bill did which was decent was to let me and a couple of others go back and carry one of our lads back to the transit; he was out cold. As we were walking back in the escort, some of the locals including the doorman were shouting, "Fair play to you lot. You're game as fuck." We shouted back, "We'll be back one day," but that day has never come.

Remember, I have had many tear ups but this one with the odds so stacked against us, we had to give it our best ever and not one of us even backed off. It didn't even enter our heads. We were in it together no matter what. Yes, we got hurt but we enjoyed every minute of it.

Is hooliganism dead at football? It's not far off due to CCTV, bans and the heavy sentencing. You just can't get away with it today. We've got some real youngsters coming through. Yes, it will never be like the old days and they know it. They're gutted but that's just the way it is.

Chapter 11
Tales Of The Unexpected
Diddy of Middlesbrough

Boro and Cardiff are very similar when it comes to the lads and there is a lot of respect for each others Firms. Here's a couple of stories from a lad called Diddy. Annis

I met the author of this book many years ago at Darlington v Cardiff and have kept in touch with him since. Annis asked me if I would like to write my account of my visits to Wales.

It was the FA Cup 1994 . When the draw was made, I was buzzing. We'd never played Cardiff. I couldn't remember the last time we'd played in Wales and they were a big name on the hooligan scene! To draw a team where we'd never been, to visit a different ground, to take on a different firm and face a new challenge - a lot of our lads were looking forward to this one!

My day started about 5:30 in the morning. A dozen of us had decided to travel with a bit of comfort and go by train to Cardiff as it was a long haul by road. We had to get the early train from Leeds and to get there on time, our only option was to start hitchhiking in twos and hope we caught our train . Dark and cold and about 6ish in the morning, the odds of us all getting there wasn't great but, somehow lucky as fuck, all of us arrived there on time, even having time to grab a bacon bun outside the station! Even when I went to the counter to pay my £42 for my train ticket, my luck was in. I put my money on the counter and the bloke pushed my tickets through the glass window but never took my money and turned away! So I just grabbed my tickets and money and was off like fuck, laughing my head off! Unbeknown to me at the time, the day was going to get even better!

The main crew of Boro lads were travelling down by coach and parking up at Newport then getting the train in. The coach was a fucking wreck and they still hadn't arrived. They were going to get into Cardiff half an hour or so behind the rest of us which wasn't what we'd been hoping! Pulling into Cardiff station virtually on 11 o'clock, the nerves started to kick in. 15 of us, not knowing what was awaiting us, were all on edge. We stepped off the train and were surprised to see only 1 or 2 police in the station who didn't bat an eyelid at us 15 walking through. Out of the station, we walked into sunny daylight not knowing which way to go. We walked straight ahead then right, looking for a boozer so we could get out of sight. As we turned right, there was a big boozer over the road and I'm not going to lie, my first thoughts were if this is full of Taffys, we're fucking dead! Anyway, there was nobody outside and lucky enough nobody inside waiting to steam out at us as we'd imagined. After all, this was Cardiff and with their reputation that's just what we thought would happen. There was another boozer over the road, The Albert. We decided to get in there, get a pint and see where the rest of the lads were.

We phoned one of the lads off the bus and they were at Newport and just about to get on the train. They were 20 minutes away. I said to my mate on the bus that I'd walk back to the station to meet them and take them to the pub we were in. Again, 50 odd lads walked out of the station and the odd copper there never batted an eyelid – result! We were now 60-70 strong and no law knew we were there and, more surprisingly up until now, we hadn't seen any Cardiff lads! More and more calls were being made between the Boro lads who were coming by car or minibus, telling them the name of the boozer we were in. All the time, there was more and more Boro arriving at the pub, boosting our numbers and our confidence! Upstairs there was a big window looking out onto the city centre. This was where quite a few of the Boro lads had gone and were sitting having a drink. It wasn't long before we spotted the first few Cardiff lads, only 3 of them but right opposite our pub.

One of them walked over and straight into the downstairs of the pub. I decided to go down and listen to what he was saying. He was by himself and talking to Doozer. I went over to introduce myself and started having a crack with him, where's your lads, etc? He was saying nobody's about at the moment as they weren't expecting us to come this early. This was something Boro had done for years, get in at eleven bells, nice and early! Anyway the Cardiff lad was sound as fuck and on his own. He was called Jonathan and again it was not our way to take liberties so he was given the respect he deserved by walking into a pub on his own, full of opposition lads. We swapped phone numbers and said we'd keep in touch especially if we had a draw here today and then they'd have to come to Boro!

Jonathan left with a shake of hands and admiration from me and Doozer. For all he knew, we could have been a bunch of wankers with no morals and slapped him about. On the other hand, we knew he was having a good look at what we had in the boozer. Unbeknown to Jonathan, most of our lads were upstairs which we both would laugh about in a year's time at Swansea! Anyway roughly an hour or so later and, by which time more and more Boro had arrived into our boozer, I was upstairs near the big front window when the shout went up, "They're here."

Stretching me neck so I could see down the High Street, there to our right I could just glimpse a mob of Cardiff heading our way. "Come on," was the shout to each other as we all pushed and shoved to get down the narrow staircase (at this point I want to state that all I can say is what I witnessed. Everyone will know when two mobs with big numbers clash, everybody has their own little stories).

Concerning the numbers on each side, opinions vary. All I can do is guess. I would have said roughly we had anything between 80-130 with Cardiff having anything between 70-100. Again, I may be way out on some opinions but it happened quickly and was 14-15 years ago. Again, if I had to guess, that's roughly what I would have said.

Anyway we were at some double doors on the left hand side of the pub. We opened them up to get out and were showered with bottles, glass, etc. The doors shut until the shout went up, "Fucking get out now!" The doors opened and out we piled, steaming straight into anybody in front of us.

We never took a backwards step and when we'd piled out, the mob of Cardiff became split into two. There was a corner opposite the pub and half of Cardiff backed off down one street and the others backed off down from where they'd come. We stayed tight and went at one mob then backed off from the ones that had stood and got done and then went at the other mob who ran back towards the station. This went on for a couple of minutes. Anyone who's been involved would know, that's quite a long time. Eventually, the mob nearest the station just melted and our attention went to the ones who were to the right. With us all together and mob handed, Cardiff didn't stand a chance. They were backed off a couple of hundred yards. We slipped down a side street and ended up right outside the Millennium stadium. Until then, I was completely unaware how close the stadium had been to us. The police arrived en masse and wrapped us all up together. By this point, we weren't too bothered as the damage had been done! We were escorted up to the ground with just a bit of verbals from the locals when we were escorted past the Ninian Park pub.

After the game, we were expecting a very hostile reception but, as we all know, the police had it all boxed off and there was very little trouble if any. We were escorted back to the station and the main crew were escorted back to Newport where rumour had it that Cardiff were waiting. The rumours were false. Boro drew 2-2 and the replay at Boro gave Cardiff the chance of revenge. With it being a midweek night game and what lads that did make the long trip north being collared on their coach on the motorway into Boro, nothing of any note occurred. Cardiff won the replay which was typical of Boro on the pitch.

A year later and Boro drew Swansea away so I rang Jonathan whose number I'd kept. Again I'd gone on the train with about 10 others. I left the train at Cardiff and met Jonathan, leaving the rest to carry on to Swansea where we'd meet back up with the rest of the Boro who'd travelled by coach, van and car. I met Jonathan and it was like we'd been mates for years. He was as sound as fuck and so were his three mates who accompanied us in the car to Swansea. When I mentioned what had happened last year with us, one of his mates turned round and said Jonathan had left our pub, gone round the Cardiff pubs trying to get a mob together saying, "C'mon, there's 50 Boro in The Albert." At that Jonathan butted in, "Yeah, I didn't fucking know there was another 50-60 of you upstairs!" At that, all of us just laughed like fuck. On arriving at Swansea, a call was made to see where our mob was. We met them in the boozer they'd occupied and we walked in to be met by all our lads, again roughly guessing between 50-80 strong. The Cardiff lads were quite impressed with our turnout considering the distance.

Everyone started chatting and Jonathan asked if we wanted him to take us to Swansea's boozer. We all nodded and agreed. Off we set, marching to their boozer. We ended up right outside the ground where Jonathan pointed, "There it is!" The name of it, I wouldn't have a clue as it's been 13-14 years now but I'm sure Jonathan or the other Cardiff lads with us that day could say. As soon as we were within yards of the pub, Jonathan and a few Boro were straight into them. By this time, the police had cottoned on to us so it was very brief. Once in the ground, we stood behind the goal. I could see some Swansea lads pointing at us as if to say, "What the fuck are Cardiff doing with Boro?" Jonathan then explained that he was well known by a lot of the Swansea firm from past experiences between the two. It was funny looking at the puzzled look on some of the Swansea faces.

After the game, there were bits and bobs of trouble with me going back to the station and Jonathan and the other three Cardiff going back to their car. Following this day, Jonathan and I became really good friends, meeting up the following year at the England v Scotland game at Euro 96 where we had a good firm down. On several occasion in the years since I've met Jonathan, I've gone down to Cardiff. Once for their playoff game at the Millennium stadium against QPR when they were promoted. Another time, away at Millwall when I have to say that the mob they took there with them that day was the biggest I've ever seen, 600-700 strong! I also went down last season v Brum but remained in the pub with 3 other Boro lads due to a ban. Every time I've been down, we've been treated with respect.

During the last 14 years or so, I've come to know through others that Jonathan, Viking and a few others are some of the main faces in Cardiff. I think I can safely say that I can count them as good, good friends and, through all the times, I've been down to Cardiff, I've met more and more lads and not once has anybody said a bad word about Boro. In fact, they've praised us since day one. My own view is and not everyone will agree with me, even some of my Boro mates, I've seen what Cardiff can muster. On their day, they must be up there with the best of them. A capital city with all the surrounding valleys etc, hence the numbers that they could sometimes pull. The day we went to Cardiff, we had the better of it big time; nobody can take that away from us. We could only do what was put in front of us and I know for a certainty that Cardiff put us up there with the best they've come across.

All in all it was a day which I'll always remember. Not only did we have a good off with one of the main firms in the country and come out on top but also for the proper friends I've made because of it.

To all of the Cardiff lads I've met over the years. Respect!

Chapter 12
A Hill Too Far
Frankie D, CCFC

My name is Frankie I've been frequenting Ninian Park since the age of 11 in the days of the old Grange End. I am now 43 and reflecting on a hooligan past where I have been banned from watching games, cautioned, thrown out of grounds and made six Court appearances. I have seen some nasty and extremely ugly incidents over the years. Although not the worst, Northampton in 1997/98 season sticks in my mind.

I think that it was primarily because it was Northampton, who do not have a history of football related violence, where the story begins. It was a hot day in Northampton. We had travelled there for the League 2 playoff semi finals, second leg. We needed to win to get to Wembley. The ground held 8,000 and our allocation was 1,500 and of that would include 500 lads. We left Cardiff around 9:00am for a 7:45pm kick-off leaving us plenty of time to look around the place and find a suitable pub. Our minibus was full. 16 lads, all game, all dressers and all veterans to football related disorder. It was a while ago but the names I remember were Rawlings, Alan, Emlyn, Little Collin, Patrick, Annis and Huwboy - apologies for leaving anyone out due to different faces being on different trips. A sell out crowd at Northampton was easily expected. It was a crucial game that was set to bring out Northampton's best mob ever and the excitement was unbearable. We arrived at Northampton around 2:00pm and quickly looked for a pub close enough to the ground but not close enough to attract the attention of the O.B. We found a suitable pub and some time later, a couple of Cardiff scarfers came in and said they had been chased by a mob of Northampton from a pub perhaps half a mile away. It was not 30 seconds and we were in the van, vexed and ready to confront Northampton for the first time today. As we arrived at the pub, we left the van in the middle of the road and headed for the pub doors. It was not long before we were spotted and an estimated 100 Northampton came out. We were not deterred by this and continued our charge towards them only to be pelted by bottles and glasses. Little Collin came the closest only to retreat under the hail of missiles.

I was surprised by their action as this was a perfect chance to give some of Cardiff's top boys a good kicking bearing in mind the numbers 7 to 1. We stayed our ground until the police arrived on horseback and with dog handlers. In a way, this saved us from being cut to pieces. We made our way to the van as quickly as possible to avoid any confrontation with the police then a funny moment came with Huwboy chasing the van as we pulled away wearing a white shirt covered in blood and tearing it off so as not to attract the attention of the Old Bill.

Diary Of The Real Soul Crew

We knew the Old Bill would come after us and therefore we needed to get our stashed booze out of the van. After perhaps a quarter of a mile, we pulled up and started walking with the cans. We knew that if the cans stayed on and the van was searched, this would be a perfect opportunity to send us back to Cardiff. The driver stayed with the van and was pulled by the police who did a stop and search, looking for anything incriminating. They found nothing and let him go. As we walked, we came to a large grass area where 20 known Cardiff casuals from Ebbw Vale were sitting. We told them about our incident at the pub. They too had had a confrontation with the same group. We sat together, discussing our course of action. Revenge was necessary. As time passed, more Cardiff joined us and our numbers were swelling. Time was pressing on and I was getting very restless. I walked off alone to do a bit of spotting and arrived at a kind of retail park with different branded burger outlets, etc. I found a pub that had a few doormen and I was convinced this had to be where they were. I approached confidently so as not to attract attention. The doormen asked me what team I supported. In my best Northampton accent, I said Northampton. I was in the pub which didn't look big from the outside but inside, I would estimate it could hold around a 1,000 people. It was packed.

I took a good look around as if I were looking for someone? The singing and chanting was really loud with lots of chants of 'England'. Lads were standing on tables waving flags. They were obviously excited and no doubt saw this as an England v Wales match as much as a Northampton v Cardiff fixture. This raised my suspicion very quickly that we may not be dealing with just Northampton fans. This was a mob of around 500 good lads with probably some Cockney lads that had come along for a pop at Cardiff. It was not long before I left this highly charged and intimidating experience. This was their mob, all grouped up so this was where we had to come to to get the off. I made my way back to the grass area to tell the lads what I had found. They quickly got to their feet. By this time, we had about 60. "Come on Cardiff. Let's do it." We left like a pack of wolves. It was a real buzz. We didn't have to walk far. 300 of them were heading towards us. It was our first toe to toe of the day. Outnumbered again, we charged towards them and punches and kicks were exchanged; then it was like the Grand National - police horses everywhere. The police pushed us back down the hill. This turned in our favour as Simmo's coach had just arrived and this swelled our numbers making things a little fairer. It was kicking off everywhere. We chased Northampton away. The Old Bill had now regrouped and batten charged us to the turnstiles where they were having no messing - into the ground we went.

In the ground, there was a lot of chanting and singing. It had a real cup tie atmosphere with a real buzz of expectancy from both sides. We were 1-0 down from the first leg and losing 1-0 on the night - the game was not in our favour so a result off the pitch was on our minds. As the game went on the Old Bill started to put on their riot gear. No doubt they sensed the mood. They then began to remove all the advertising boards; something I can say I've never seen before.

Lakey had about 30 of his lads and they were making their way towards their end of the ground. We followed but the Old Bill didn't catch on straight away. When they did, they locked the gates and stopped more Cardiff leaving but about 40 of us managed to get out. It wasn't enough but we had no option - we walked around to their end. The Old Bill had other ideas and headed us towards a grass bank where some 800 ticket less Northampton were watching the game. It was inevitable that we would get a good row. This was a situation where most teams would run. We didn't. We are Cardiff and are fearless. This was one of the best positions a hooligan could find himself in. A mob right in front of you and your adrenaline pumping. A stand off ensued with our 40 to their 150. Then Annis appeared and steamed in to them. Around five Northampton attacked him. I backed him up. It then kicked off and there were bodies everywhere. It seemed to go on forever. One of my most memorable toe to toes ever.

It was inevitable the volume of numbers would get the better of us and we were forced down the hill. It was a scrap that was to leave us battered and bruised but it wasn't over. We then regrouped and charged back up the hill towards them. Anyone that's been to Northampton will know how steep this hill is. We were knackered just climbing the hill. We then had our second toe to toe with only our small numbers but we gave it our best shot. We did feel we had been done. Once again, we were forced back down the hill and we were exhausted. I remember Emlyn shouting, "Come on lads, one more time." Up the hill we went; we were like a depleted army but we were not going to lose face.

I remember making my third trip up the hill when, from the distance, we heard chants of "Soul Crew." The game had finished and the gates were open. We gained instant strength. It was now kicking off everywhere and Northampton were running but there always seemed to be smaller Northampton mobs appearing. The battles went on for around half an hour before the police finally took control.

I arrived back at the minibus where I was greeted by our boys with ripped shirts, cuts, bruises. It was a good day out. We left Northampton and headed home and stopped on the way at a pub in Silverstone where we sat down and discussed the day's events. We virtually all admitted that if it were a boxing match then Northampton beat our 40 on the hill on points. We were convinced that it was not just a Northampton mob. We know that London mobs turn up anywhere so that they can to take on Cardiff. Northampton wouldn't have that good a mob. I felt our 40 could hold their heads up with pride. We done well.

BBC NEWS

More 'thugs' banned from Cardiff City 8 August, 2002

Arrests at Cardiff City matches have trebled

Cardiff City football has one of the worst records for hooliganism in the football league, according to Home Office figures.

Courts banned 125 Bluebirds fans from going to matches at home and abroad last season, in a year which saw an upsurge in violence in and around grounds.

The number of banning orders was the highest of any other club as football's authorities attempted a high-profile crackdown on hooligans ahead of the World Cup in Japan and Korea.

Hooliganism figures from Home Office

Arrests at Cardiff games: 129
Cardiff fans' banning orders: 125
Arrests at Swansea games: 7
Arrests at Wrexham games: 11

The Association of Chief Police Officers has named Cardiff City as one of the "problem clubs" in Division Two, despite a pledge by its chairman, Sam Hammam that he would crackdown on its thuggish supporter element.

But the picture for other league teams in Wales is not as grim - Swansea City had only 7 arrests, down from 72 the previous season, and Wrexham just 11, also well down.

Home Office statistics show Cardiff City is a contender for the top place in the sport's hooliganism league.

The number of arrests at Cardiff games more than doubled from 40 in league games to 100, and 129 in all competitions, while overall

arrests for football-related arrests during the 2001-02 season fell by six per cent.

Chapter 13
My Story
Dave Chappell, Crystal Palace

By the time this is published and being read by you, I will be living in New Zealand and all the fun and games from my time on the terraces will be a fond memory. A bit about me. I'm 30 years old. I was born, bred and still living in Bedford until the beginning of this year. Coming from Bedford. my team should have been Luton Town but no. I ended up following Crystal Palace. This is all thanks to when I was 11 years old and my parents took me to America. We flew with Virgin who, at the time, sponsored the Palace shirt. Well, I wanted the club shirt due to it having 'Fly Virgin' on the front. From there, a love affair began which will never die.

As I started to go more and more to games, I started to recognise and eventually talk to and drink with people who were Palace's firm. Good lads like Braddy from Stevenage, Wayne from Whadden were two in particular. I'm still good mates with them and would want them by my side in any situation. In my chapter for this book, I'm not claiming to be a top boy or hard man. I've fallen, I've stood, I've run, I've not run, I loved the buzz plain and simple. Obviously clothes were a big part of it, as well. I started out in the usual way with Ralph Lauren, Stone Island, Burberry, etc. I now prefer things like APC, 6876, 80's Casuals and YMC; no labels on show, nice, plain and simple stuff rounded off with a nice pair of Addidas originals. It's a shame to see all the Stone (clone) Island warriors, lads who don the jumper or coat and think they are in the football factory, fucking idiots!

Anyway onto how I met the author of this book......

I went to Poland with some Palace lads for an England qualifier and we travelled by coach from Victoria. On our coach was a girl from Manchester called Ceri who followed Liverpool and Cardiff City. We became friends and she offered to take me to see Cardiff when we returned home. Her offer was accepted and I went with her to Cambridge Utd v Cardiff City in the old division 3. The result was a 2-2 draw with Cardiff equalising in the final minute sending the travelling fans into raptures. After the game, we went for a drink with a few of the Soul Crew and I couldn't have been made to feel more welcome. To be honest, I was nervous about going, what with the reputation they had and especially being English. No need to worry though, they were all great with me.

Annis was at the game but had gone straight home. My first meeting with him would come at Ninian Park one Sunday afternoon. This was going to be a real baptism of fire. I was off to see Cardiff v Swansea. Ceri sorted out tickets and myself and two mates from Bedford, Percy and Cunno, set off to the Welsh capital on a Saturday morning for a night on the piss and a day at the match. The night went by with a boozy haze and, believe me, full English breakfast was required the next morning before heading off to the game.

The walk down Penarth Road towards the ground was a long one, hung-over and full of anticipation for the three of us from Bedford. We timed it right. As we arrived, Swansea were being escorted in on their buses. These were duly barracked by the Cardiff faithful for being gypos. I have to say I agreed.

We were being introduced to so many people, it all became a blur in the end. I couldn't put a name to a face. We made our way to the Bob Bank and a real cauldron of hate it was. One person I was introduced to was Annis and, from that day, we became firm friends and I will class him as one of my best mates now. From what I remember from the game, it finished 0-0. The Jacks made a half hearted attempt to get into the Bob Bank from the Grange end which was never going to happen due to fencing and the police. A few Sunderland lads who were down with Annis, pulled one of the gates open to let Cardiff onto the pitch. It came to nothing as the Old Bill, who were there in numbers, sorted it out within seconds. There's no harm with trying. What stood out for me being at this game was the sheer number of lads Cardiff had out. It was amazing and again everyone was friendly and welcoming. The game ended, the Jacks were put on their buses and escorted home while we made our way to Cardiff Central to get home. All in all, an eye opener as I'd never seen so much hatred between two sets of fans and a great weekend.

One thing I am going to put to words to defend Cardiff is that there is a book out called 'Swansea Jacks'. In it, the author describes how Swansea attack the exchange pub in Cardiff. This they did, yes. But what they fail to mention was that 7 or 8 Cardiff who came out of the pub backed off at least triple their number down the road. I have only seen this on video but I know what I saw, so please don't talk bollocks. I have another bone of contention with the book and I shall write about that later.

After the Swansea game, I started to stay in touch with Annis more and more which meant I started attending more games with him. Home and away, I've been with Cardiff with a thousand lads and I've been with twenty. No matter what odds, they have always obliged and in my opinion have never been bullies. I've seen them give quite a few lads walkovers. They are hard but fair. Look for it at Ninian Park and your fucked. Mind your own business, don't act simple much like Millwall.

Ah, Millwall. The boys from Bermondsey. What a prospect. First game of the season, Millwall at home. I had to have a ticket for this one. How the game wasn't rescheduled, I'll never know. Still, I didn't want to miss it. A ticket was purchased in the Bob Bank and off I set. I stayed at Annis's on the Friday night in order to get to the City Centre early Saturday morning. We had been told that Millwall were due to arrive early. We were in the city for 9:00am. About this time, the first train pulled in from London with 30-40 Millwall on; they were run within minutes of entering the town centre but it wasn't Millwall's main lads, it was just kids. When the second train arrived, different story. This was the true Millwall, all men, no kids. Fuck me, they looked the business. Millwall were put into Sam's bar and a few other bars in Mill Lane and surrounded by police. While Millwall were being escorted to the bars, around 400-500 Cardiff were battling the police on Penarth road to get to their London rivals. This was fighting with the police like I hadn't seen before. This was proper Cardiff, using planks of wood, missiles anything they could lay their hands on while Millwall took the piss from outside the bars.

Myself and Annis managed to stay inside the city centre and were watching Millwall. You could see Cardiff charging towards the bridge to the city centre. Millwall were eventually escorted off to the ground once the roads ahead had been cleared of Cardiff fans. We were informed to get to the Severn Oaks Park as Cardiff were going to ambush the escort. This possibly would have worked if the police hadn't tried to land a helicopter in the middle of the two mobs. The police escort managed to get Millwall into the ground without anymore trouble. Inside, it was an evil atmosphere with both sets of fans hurling coins, lighters, etc at each other as well as the usual numerous insults. The game finished in a 1-1 draw with both goals coming from the penalty spot. I couldn't wait for the game to finish to see what would happen after. When the final whistle went, for some reason the police allowed us to exit via the back of the Grange End. This meant more missile throwing from hundreds of young casuals as we were walking behind the Millwall end. The police were trying to contain Millwall inside while Cardiff were gathering in serious numbers outside the ground. The numbers must have been 1,000-1,500 lads, all waiting ready for Millwall to come out and, when they eventually did, it went mental. Millwall came from underneath the Grandstand and those that came out first were some of the gamest I've ever seen. Cardiff were like locusts, all over them, attacking them and forcing them back into the ground. The Millwall who came out first were hammered and well and truly fucked. As always, the police eventually separated both sides and had the unenviable job of getting the City fans to disperse. The police kept making baton charges into us on Sloper Road and Penarth Road, the result of which was some bruised legs for yours truly. We made our way back to the city centre and had a few beers; another good day with Cardiff coming to an end.

Since that game and thanks to Annis, I've got to know a top Millwall lad called Para Paul who met Annis many years ago while staying at a hotel Annis had. I have been with him on various occasions to Millwall games and again been made most welcome. He was even my chauffeur for my now wife when we were married - Thanks Paul.

Well, in the Swansea Jacks book they say how they drunk at Millwall last season - wrong they drunk at London Bridge not Bermondsey then they had an escort to the New Den and came in the coward's way. Yes, they had a mob and attacked the police but, believe me, if Millwall had wanted, they would have destroyed Swansea. Obviously they weren't worth the hassle. I was there and saw it first hand; it was nothing like as described in their book.

I did have an encounter with Swansea and it happened to be my stag do in 2001 in Newquay. All in all, about 35 of us attended. There was a good mix of lads from Palace, Cardiff, a lad Browny from Ilkeston who was a Derby lad and my mates from Bedford. Well, it turned into the usual stag do on the Friday with me being paraded around the town, dressed up like Captain Caveman and everyone in a very drunken state, enjoying ourselves with no trouble. That was until the Saturday night. On the Saturday night, myself and two Cardiff lads Lakey and Ritchie from Blackwood were in one of the bars in the town. The rest of the lads were in various bars and restaurants further down the road and had arranged to meet up with us in this particular pub (the name escapes me after all these years). Anyway, the three of us were having a drink and it was full of the usual hen party's, stag do's and people having a good time. Then the DJ started to shout out that the 'Jack Army' were in the 'House'. All eyes darted onto the dance floor and Lakey went over, took a look and came back saying it was some of their main lads. The phones started ringing in the rest of the lads pockets as news quickly spread that Swansea were here and it was all systems go. Our lot found two columns outside the main doors to the pub. It was like a wedding where the bride and groom walk in between and are showered in confetti. Well, Swansea were the happy couple and we were the guests. It was Lakey who called them on and the next thing, they knew was they were coming out to a barrage of punches. No confetti here, just fists. They came out game as fuck. Unfortunately, the first one bumped into my mate Mr T from Stevenage and he was a goner. When the rest of their lads saw the situation, they were trying to get back into the pub. It was all over too quickly. No-one was too badly hurt. They just didn't know what was outside. Anyway, there was loads of commotion going on with the bouncers at this point. They didn't realise that they were dealing with a football mob and not a load of surfers. The next thing we knew, the police were coming. Annis had been recognised by some of the Swansea and there were cameras in the pub which we, in our state, had failed to notice. Needless to say, we all left very quickly. Some stayed in the hotel. Some of us went and changed and went back out. There was no more fun that night. Just a load more beer and drunkenness.

Mansfield away with Cardiff, last game of the season was a promotion party for City and they received a paltry allocation of away tickets because the ground only had three sides due to redevelopment. At the time, I became the ticket man phoning Mansfield nearly everyday for more tickets, telling them we were on a stag do in Nottingham that weekend and wanted to see the game. I ended up with about 40 tickets due to demand and was on first name terms with the women in the ticket office.

Forest made a show at the game with around 50 of their lads suddenly turning up out of the blue and wading straight in. Cardiff duly obliged and a police line was put in to separate us both. There were lads from Cardiff in the home end so it felt like a home game to Cardiff. The result escapes me but it was me being chased around Mansfield town centre after the game that stayed in my mind. I had said my 'goodbyes' to Annis and the boys and had gone into town to get something to eat. I had a luminous yellow coat on and was recognised from the ground by some locals and was forced to do my best Linford Christie impression as shouts of 'get that Welsh bastard' came from behind me. I'm sure if I had stopped and explained that I was English and a Palace fan they would have been more lenient. Never mind, it cost me £30 to escape in a taxi, to Nottingham. The jacket was cast aside in the back of the wardrobe as looking like an Irish navvy was not good anymore.

Spurs away in the Carling Cup 3rd round; brilliant, another must go game. I went down to London and met Lakey and a few of his mates in the daytime, had a mooch around some shops before making our way around the dreaded M25 to Tottenham. We met up with Annis's car load and a mini bus of lads on the A10. After a couple of beers, it was time to go to White Heart Lane. I went in the car with Annis, Jo, Michael and a lad called Brian. We parked up in one of the many housing estates near the ground and started to walk to White Hart Lane. Phone calls were coming in thick and fast, saying Spurs had a top mob out and were attacking Cardiff at every opportunity. Darkness had now set in and you could sense trouble; everything around felt dodgy. We were walking parallel to a park and could see a pub called 'The Artichoke' in the distance with a lot of figures milling around outside. It was decided that I would walk ahead and, if they were Spurs, then with my accent I would talk and Annis and Co could walk on. We were well outnumbered and would have been fucked. Fortunately it turned out to be Cardiff; pleasantries were exchanged and we carried onto the ground.

The phone calls were right. Spurs had a top mob out. All colours, shapes and sizes filled the streets around the ground. The police were holding them back, allowing Cardiff fans to get into the ground. Unfortunately for us, the Met decided they were going to make our group of five walk through the Spurs mob and all the way around the ground to 'teach us a lesson' to get to the away end. One copper saw sense though eventually, after much arguing and allowed us through - phew! As we approached the turnstiles, about 150 ticket less Cardiff fans kicked a gate open and all got in. In the ground, all the talk was on Cardiff being picked off in dribs and drabs. The game was terrible and Spurs won 1-0, final whistle went. Right, let's get out. We were told we were going to be escorted on the way out of the ground and fortunately it was the direction of the car. If we had parked anywhere else, it could have been a dodgy walk. Anyway, out onto the street and Spurs were being held back both sides of the road by the police. All of a sudden, the roar we all knew went up and, fuck it, the Spurs mob began attacking the police. Cardiff joined in and attacked the police and moved towards the Spurs mob. It was going off everywhere with loads of running battles. Fights were kicking off in the car park outside the ground. It went mad. Cardiff were now together and there must have been at least 600 lads who were all trying to get at Spurs.

There was too much going on all around to focus on one thing. The Old Bill were desperately trying to get Cardiff moving back onto the coaches but it just wasn't happening. There was too much going on. There was a large mob of Spurs trying to get through a park on our left. They were being monitored by a helicopter and Cardiff were trying to get into the park to stop any ambush. Every side road and alley had police at the end of it. Spurs were trying everything to get at us; it was manic. Full marks to Spurs, they were awesome that night and certainly gave us as good as they got. Honours, even in my book!

When we returned to the car, we were all buzzing as to what a top night it had been.

Diary Of The Real Soul Crew

I will say thanks to Annis and Michael for certainly stopping me from getting mugged at St Albans train station where they dropped me off, thanks for noticing the lads following me - Cheers.

Chapter 14
Hooligans in Uniform
Big Sam, CCFC

My name is Sam and I am from the Merthyr area of South Wales. I was asked to give you my version of events when my club Cardiff City played Stoke City in a promotion/relegation clash in April 2000. I was one of the thousands of Cardiff fans who travelled that day along with many and I mean many from the Valleys of South Wales where Cardiff have a huge following. Merthyr, Rhondda, Aberdare, Pontypridd, Tredegar, Rhymney, Ebbw Vale, Mountain Ash, Maesteg - all big Valley towns with a big Cardiff following. This is my and others' versions of the events that took place that day. No lies, no bullshit, the truth of how we were treated by a police force who were a disgrace to their uniform and the South Wales press and TV companies who, in their own way, were just as bad as the police and in my mind, wankers the lot of them.

The people who were at the Stoke game that day all have similar stories to tell. I just happened to have been asked to tell mine with a little help from a few of my mates. Here we go then, make of it what you will.

Right lads, we all have to go to another fucking relegation battle on behalf of our beloved Cardiff City. This time, we were playing Stoke City who were going for promotion big time. If we are relegated, it's back to the dungeon Division 4. To us old bastards, it would be for the 3rd, 4th, 5th time? God knows. I've lost count of how many relegations we have had over the years. Apart from being a top Division 1 team. Stoke have a well respected 'Firm' called 'The Naughty Forty'. Well respected not just by Cardiff but by everyone who knows anything about real football lads. For this one, everyone was off their arses and off we jolly well went.

The game itself was put back to a Sunday afternoon with a 2:00pm kick-off on police advice in case of trouble and the funny thing was that most of the trouble that day was caused by the police themselves, the wankers. As the game was on a Sunday, most of the Valley lads could not get to Cardiff early because of the trains (you have more chance of winning the Lottery than getting a train early to Cardiff on a Sunday morning) never mind getting one back home. So it was coaches for us lot then, loads of them. I spoke to my great mate, Desy from Barry and they were taking coaches as well. This could and should be a very interesting day.

Years ago, the Valleys and Cardiff lads never used to get on and I personally used to hate that but it's different now, thank fuck as we all support the City. The Barry lads and us have always been great mates and always will be. Funny story is that Annis and myself go way back and have been there and seen it all. I'm a

Valley lad and he's a Cardiff lad but we both support the same team and that's how it should be. Many of the Valley boys are ex-miners, ex-steelworkers, loads of ex's that's because everything's been fucking shut down. South Wales in general is a working class area and not very affluent at that. There is a huge support for the City in the Valleys and most of the lads don't give a fuck about anything else except the City, Beer, Women and a tear up; there is fuck all else to do. Watching the City good or bad, mostly bad, was and still is a release from everyday things and I should imagine it's the same at any working class clubs like Stoke, Millwall, Pompey, Boro, Wolves, W.H.U, Sheff Wed and Utd, Sunderland, Hull, etc. I myself have personally always felt cheated by my club, the police, Welsh FA and the media, especially the fucking one-eyed, Rugby-orientated, bullshitting Welsh media and also by my club for selling any decent players we ever had and various chairman shafting us big time. The police for treating us like fucking terrorists. I've lost count of 'bubble' games we have had and treating us like shit. It's no wonder we have played up over the years. The Welsh FA are a sack of shit. The sooner we come under the English FA umbrella the better. As for the Welsh media, they are obsessed with the egg (Rugby) and slate my club and our fans for any little incident. The reason for this little rant will become clearer as the day at Stoke unfolds.

We had two coaches from Merthyr. All the usual suspects were there, Meathead, The Neck, Bonker, Ritchy, Mad Jack Lewis, Taylor, Ted, Sapic, Carlton, The Foley Clan, Stud, Hooker who has sadly passed away since, Skull and his crew and many of the Valley Soul Crew lads. On the way, we met many other coaches from all over South Wales. The weather was fine and everyone was confident of what we were about to face but some of the actions of this particular police force surprised even the more 'experienced' campaigners amongst the lads. Off we go then. We leave Merthyr and onto the heads of the valleys road, M50, M5, M6. Everyone on the coach is bouncing. Bonker gets up and says, "Anyone who runs gets a fucking kicking and can fucking walk home." Everyone laughs, "Let's have it". Can't wait to get to Stoke. We get calls on our phones to say the Old Bill are waiting for us so we take our coaches off the motorway to a place called Stone. We find a boozer called The Post House or Post Inn - none of us can remember the bloody name of the pub. We have a few beers; no trouble, nice and quiet. The pub was shut when we first arrived. As we were nice and early, after an hour or so, we mount up and head for Stoke. When we get off the motorway, there's a number of roundabouts and as we approach one of these, we see them fucking hundreds of police; they were everywhere. There were Cardiff coaches and vans in the lay-bys and on the inside lane as far as you could see. The police were everywhere and I mean everywhere.

The police were holding us in a lay-by, hard shoulder and inside lane of a dual carriageway. Don't really know how many coaches or vans were there but there were loads. We must have been held there for 20-30 minutes and everyone was getting really angry with the police when they started to move us out. We were not at all happy with the police action but at least we were on our way. As we approached another roundabout, the Britannia Stadium was straight over and all the coaches and vans and the law go right. Where the fuck are we going now? By now, it's around 1:30pm and the game was due to kick-off in 30 minutes. The law then

Simmo with Sam Hammam at Ninian Park.

Gwyn Davies, Valley Rams at Barnsley.

HATE - Cardiff supporters try to taunt their Millwall rivals at the New Den.

Mark Gregor, QPR

Cardiff's Mob trying to get at Man Utd when they played in the Millennium Stadium.

Simmo and some of the lads in the services on one of their many away trips on the battle bus.

Simmo at Blackpool away doing nothing wrong but,
once again, the police are fully watching.

Valley Lads, Gwyn, Mr Williams & Taffy

*Big Sam with his shades on outside Ninian Park with his mates,
Neck, Mac, Vince and a couple of other lads.*

*Gilroy Shaw
(Gilly)
of Wolves.*

Cardiff in an escort being watched by Gregors (Mark Gregor) and some QPR.

Cardiff Lads being held back by riot police in Camp Street, Wolverhampton.
Wolves v Cardiff, 2006.
After this match, Cardiff fans were banned from attending Wolves again.

Frankie and me visiting a prisoner of war camp in Prague on my 2006 Stag Do.

July 21ˢᵗ, 2006 with those who could get up for breakfast on my Stag Do in Prague. Bradley, Frankie D, Dave (C Palace), Pete, Dave, Tony, Paul (Millwall), myself, Topman.

Millwall (Para Paul) & Man Utd (Bradley) at my wedding, 2006

Neath lads going to Peterborough in the FA Cup.

The Zulus at Ninian Park, 2006. 150 of them arrive at 3:15pm.

The Zulus, 2006. They made their presence felt but didn't arrive to 3:15pm.

Two youth firms
EXH N° 5
10th February 07
Coventry .v. Cardiff.

Cardiff at Coventry, 10th February 2007 - Two Youth Firms, EXH No 5

Chelsea Pat and myself

A bunch of Cardiff lads.
Section A of the Grandstand outside Ninian Park, 2008

Jonathan Evans and his son Daniel, my godson.

(Below) myself and Dave Chappell, a Crystal Palace lad.

A group of diehard City lads who preferred to be at the City when the eggheads
were playing up the road.
Tonto, Big Sam, Corky, Mac, Simmo, Dave, Vince, Simon & myself.

Dave, Diddy and his son (Boro Lads) and myself in the Algarve 2008
Tournament. All mates. How times have changed.

Newport at Cardiff, 2008

Newport at Cardiff, 2008

Wembley 2008. Some lads still fly the flag.

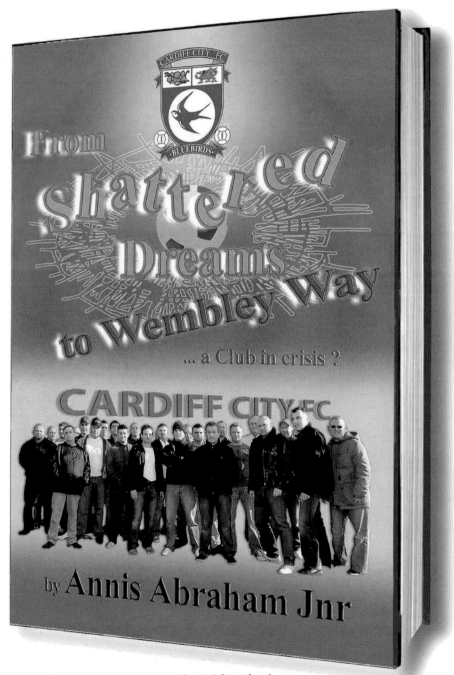

Annis' first book,
'From Shattered Dreams to Wembley Way', released 28th June, 2008.
On sale at www.headhunterbooks.co.uk.

direct all coaches and vans into a huge compound which was a piece of ground at a place called Trentham Gardens. The number of police there was unbelievable and the vast majority of them were in full riot gear. You could only see the tosser's eyes. This place was like an internment camp for terrorists or illegal immigrants. It was the nearest thing to ethnic cleansing without being fucking shot. There must have been 700-800 of us, probably more. They had this piece of equipment like they use at the airport where you walk through and an alarm goes off to check for metal objects. This metal detector for want of a better word was placed in the middle of this waste ground. The police were obviously hoping that we would all walk through the detector, all 800 of us mind and maybe find knives, axes, machetes, guns, rocket launchers and maybe a fucking tank, the stupid twats. Our bus was way back in the queue and there was no way we were going to make the kick-off as it was 2:00pm already. A copper gets on the bus and tells us that the kick-off had been delayed by 30 minutes. On some of the coaches up front, the lads started piling off the buses/coaches, they stripped off and started running bollock naked through the metal detector. It was fucking hilarious and mad at the same time. As this was happening, Des from Barry jumped on our bus to say we were 1-0 down in the game. The game? The Old Bill had just said it had been put back by 30 minutes, the lying bastards. Fuck this. Everyone piled off the coaches and vans and it went potty. For all their armour, no-one gave a fuck about them and it was chaos for a while. After what seemed like an age but was only probably a minute, a no-man's land appeared; how the hell that happened I ain't got a clue. An inspector appeared and said to get back on the transport and they will take us to the ground. He was called every name under the sun and he said there had been a misunderstanding, wrong information, etc. Now we may not be the most intelligent set of fans but, for fucks sake, how thick do they think we really are. The lying twats.

On one of the vans, they found some tools. It was the guy's work van and I know him well. He's from Aberdare and he had forgotten to empty it, a bit dopey but it happens. They found Stanley blades, hammers, shovels and a fucking huge disk cutter. The law and press later had a field day with the disk cutter incident. Let's be fair. The disk cutter was as big as the bloke that owned it. How the hell could he get it through the turnstile? And, if by some act of God, he did, what was he going to do with it in the ground? Chop a fucking stand down? I ask you.

Anyway, we eventually get to the Britannia Stadium and it was half-time. Fucking great, 1-0 down; could it get any worse? Well, it sure could and would. We get off the coaches and vans and we get searched yet again. Fuck me, are they all queer up here or something? At the same time, the lads on the trains were arriving and they had had similar problems to us. There were around 400 of them. With our lot, there must have been 1200-1300 Cardiff outside the ground at half-time and people wonder why we were angry. Finally we were in the ground with the second half already started and we were still 1-0 down and staring relegation in the face again. I don't think most of our lads gave a toss after the way we were treated by the law. There was a lot of posturing and gesturing and a few surges by both sets of lads during the second half but nothing really happened. One incident summed up the day so far which was the police in particular and their attitude. We went

2-0 down but managed to pull a goal back, 2-1 and we were on top when we had a corner with just 5-10 minutes to go. A wall of riot police were facing us all along the bye-line and Andy Legg, City's fullback could not take the corner because a fucking great big police horse stood on the corner flag and the twat would not move. I ask you. We were all waiting for the horse to cross the ball. It was total chaos and we end up losing 2-1.

Everyone is in a foul mood and out we go. Anyone who has been to the Britannia Stadium will know that the coaches, vans, etc are parked in a compound which is fenced up all the way around as you come out of the ground. To the left, there is a high banking maybe 40 feet above the compound. A lot of the Stoke fans were up there, chucking objects into the packed solid compound. A few of us made it to the perimeter fencing and were trying to pull it down. A few of the Stoke lads were trying to get it down as well but the riot police waded in. Myself and Bonker were battered by them, by truncheons. I had my knee cap split open and was also gassed and Bonker was truncheoned on the back and head and gassed. Then it really kicked off. The lads had had enough of the riot police and attacked them, scattering them everywhere. The police regrouped and attacked Cardiff and drove the lads back. It was total chaos. This time Cardiff were organised and attacked the riot police again, driving them up the banking and along the top of the fence. Fuck me, the riot police were on their toes. The horrible bastards received what they deserved. Hours later, everyone's rounded up and taken out of Stoke. One amazing thing about the day. I don't think there was one punch thrown between any Cardiff or Stoke lads. Totally amazing.

Finally to round off a really mad day, our coach was on the Heads of The Valleys Road approaching Merthyr on the way home when it caught fire and I mean on fire. The back wheels were ablaze and the driver pulled into a petrol station. Jesus Christ, how dull is that? I've never seen 50 lads get off a coach so quick in all my life. We were like rats leaving a sinking ship. Emergency door, shit house door, out through the sunroof, it was abandon ship time. Looking back, we laugh about it but at the time we shit ourselves.

Over the next few days and weeks, our fans were slaughtered in the press and local TV. I also believe Stoke fans had the same bad press but the truth of the matter is the policing that day was of the lowest calibre. They were to blame for 90% of the problems, the police's attitude, their ignorance, lies and complete mis-management along with their bully boy tactics caused the chaotic scenes at Trentham Gardens, inside the Britannia Stadium and outside the Stadium. They were nothing but a disgrace to their uniform.

Ten months later the arrests started. I personally had a dawn raid. Seven charming officers, two of which were from Stoke came through my front door, took me to Llanishen nick where I was charged and bailed. There were a few who were raided. I'm not 100% sure but around 60-70 were done. The real sickner was our glamorous South Wales Press printing photos (mug shots) of Cardiff supporters on the front pages of their papers for days. Funny, I always thought you were innocent in this country until proven guilty. Again I'm led to believe the Stoke lads had the same treatment as our lot. Isn't it strange two working class sets of fans treated like shit?

The South Wales press were a disgrace. Good people lost their jobs through wankers and when it came to Court, some of the banning orders were unreal. Anything from 3-10 years and for what? For complete mis-management by a pig of a police force that day that had treated us and probably the Stoke lads like shit and with complete disregard for human rights. No wonder the lads reacted like they did. You get less for murdering someone in this country.

Looking back at that day, we lost and were relegated three days later, again! Stoke went up. Both sets of fans were hammered in the Courts and press. They called it one of the worst cases of football violence ever. When in truth, the biggest hooligans that day were the fucking police. Decades of experience has taught me that all police forces contain good and bad elements but, on that day, we definitely came up against the worst Stoke had to offer.

Cardiff fans in violent flare-up

POLICE were today studying CCTV footage after violence flared during yesterday's Stoke City 2-1 win over Cardiff City when supporters tore down security fences and threw coins and missiles from the stands.

The game was the subject of a heavy police presence following threats of violence posted on the Internet by rival fans. Staffordshire police said it deployed 600 officers and made 20 arrests before kick-off, mostly for alcohol-related offences.

A police spokesman said searches of travelling fans' coaches and at the Britannia Stadium turned up various potential weapons, including a circular saw and 100 Stanley knife blades.

During the match, Stoke boosted their chances of a Second Division play-off place as they overcame their relegation-threatened rivals in front of 14,000 spectators.

About 2,000 Cardiff fans were expected to travel to the Potteries for the fixture, but police had warned anyone without a ticket to stay away.

A search area was set up at the ground to stop troublemakers bringing in weapons, and the empty section of seating between rival fans was widened and filled with several layers of security fencing.

At one stage during the match, the police presence prevented Cardiff's Andy Legg from taking a corner as mounted police officers were in the way.

During play, several seats were ripped up and coins and drink were thrown at police.

A police spokesman said the police operation had been a tremendous success, adding: "The aim was to minimise the opportunity for disorder and when it occurred to resolve it effectively, with the minimum use of force and the minimum number of injuries."

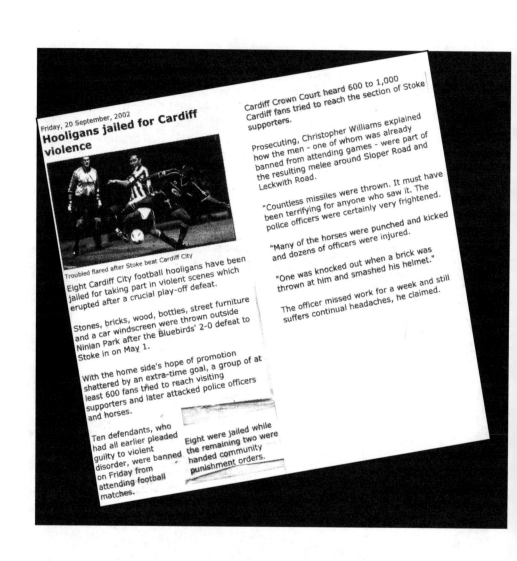

Friday, 20 September, 2002

Hooligans jailed for Cardiff violence

Troubled flared after Stoke beat Cardiff City

Eight Cardiff City football hooligans have been jailed for taking part in violent scenes which erupted after a crucial play-off defeat.

Stones, bricks, wood, bottles, street furniture and a car windscreen were thrown outside Ninian Park after the Bluebirds' 2-0 defeat to Stoke in on May 1.

With the home side's hope of promotion shattered by an extra-time goal, a group of at least 600 fans tried to reach visiting supporters and later attacked police officers and horses.

Ten defendants, who had all earlier pleaded guilty to violent disorder, were banned on Friday from attending football matches.

Eight were jailed while the remaining two were handed community punishment orders.

Cardiff Crown Court heard 600 to 1,000 Cardiff fans tried to reach the section of Stoke supporters.

Prosecuting, Christopher Williams explained how the men - one of whom was already banned from attending games - were part of the resulting melee around Sloper Road and Leckwith Road.

"Countless missiles were thrown. It must have been terrifying for anyone who saw it. The police officers were certainly very frightened.

"Many of the horses were punched and kicked and dozens of officers were injured.

"One was knocked out when a brick was thrown at him and smashed his helmet."

The officer missed work for a week and still suffers continual headaches, he claimed.

Chapter 15
My Thoughts On Cardiff
Gilly Shaw

I met Gilly in Euro 2000 in Brussels after the fight I had in the square with Blackburn. I had gone for a drink outside a bar called O'Reillys, Gilly was standing there with about 25 Wolves lads, Cardiff have a lot of respect for Wolves which goes right back to the 80's. Since I've been visiting Molineux, Wolves have always had a good firm out for Cardiff.

Gilly saw me outside O'Reillys and came over and introduced himself and said, "Fair play on you Taffy for standing up to those bully bastard Blackburn fans." We had a drink together and through numerous people have managed to keep in contact ever since.

Annis.

A lad who works for security down the Molineux spoke to Annis at the Wolves v Cardiff game 2008 and, as they both knew me, I was once again put in contact with Annis. He asked me if I would write my thoughts on Cardiff. I had no hesitation as I have a lot of respect for Cardiff. I also remember Annis in Brussels who had been caught up in the mayhem after he'd had a fight with some Blackburn loud mouths. The police had arrived outside a bar from which Annis had been dragged and dumped on the floor. He made out that he was choking but I suppose he must have been at some point with all the tear gas the Old Bill were using. The Old Bill released their grip on him and stood back to give him space to get air. That was it. He took his chance and leapt to his feet and was off. Mind you, he didn't get very far before he was pounced on and wrestled to the ground. This time the coppers took no chance and were almost sitting on him to hold him down. Nazi Germany springs to mind on how we were all treated. It was a fucking disgrace.

Cardiff for years have had a top firm. I have also seen them up close as a bit of a neutral when a few years ago they played a mid week cup game against Spurs in London. I went down there. Cardiff had an awesome firm, likewise so did the Yids who at one point I swear must have had a 700 strong mob out on the street. Love them or hate them, there is no denying that both clubs can pull a top firm when needed and by saying this I'm not sucking up to anyone. It was going off big time before and after the game and I'd give it honours even, you couldn't split the two mobs. In the last couple of years, Cardiff have also came up to our place and turned out in huge numbers. It had been billed as an England v Wales game and afterwards it went mental with the Old Bill totally struggling to keep the warring fans apart. Fair play to them, they turned up and came looking for it.

Diary Of The Real Soul Crew

In the old Forth Division, Cardiff turned up massive at our place. They turned up 200 of them at 11:00am at the train station. Our lot were still in their beds so no-one was out ready for them. The Old Bill quickly seized them and escorted them to the ground. The gates didn't open until around 1:00pm so the coppers just put a ring of men around them to stop them moving. Hundreds of Wolves gathered within sight of them but no-one could get at each other. We've played Newport and Wrexham and they would also give you a good row, however Cardiff are the top firm to come out of Wales in my opinion.

The Soul Crew are a top firm. You know they are guaranteed to turn up, they'd never let you down.

Gilly Shaw, Author of 'Running With A Pack Of Wolves'

Chapter 16
Burberry, Bristol and Bullshit
Glenn V, CCFC

I've known Glenn and his family for many a year and yes, Glenn does favour the casual look with all the latest designer labels but he never was an out and out thug. Here he tells his true account of his wrongful arrest and Court appearances. Glenn is the type of lad that gets on with everyone he meets and is well liked by all the lads. Here in his own words is his experiences of being set up for something he never done and played no part in . Remember it could happen to you!
Annis.

I had been to a few games here and there with some lads from school in the early 80's but started going regularly to games, home and away, in 1985 just after leaving school. We were a really poor team at the time after consecutive relegations and we didn't have a great following, home or away. As we had low crowds, a lot of lads at the time got to know each other, seeing the same faces week in week out. I had obviously heard of Annis as he owned Caesars Nightclub in the centre of Cardiff. You hear stories but once I came to know the man well, he was a genuine honest man who loved and still loves the City more than anyone I know. I have been on numerous trips with Annis, home and away and he is a good laugh and funny character.

I was going down with some lads from North Cardiff and you meet others and it goes on from there. Football is a great way of building lifetime friendships. I started to drink with some lads in the Grand Vaults in Westgate Street and we would go there before and after every home game. We called ourselves the BRAT boys for some reason; British Rail Alcoholic Tribe. Don't ask me why. Lads from different areas of Cardiff and Penarth. Budgie (RIP) whom I was in school with and at 13 had a full grown beard! H (Partridge), Sully, Jenko and Elts from Penarth, Paul Simmo and numerous others. There were a few other groups at the time, The Docks boys, Booze Crew, Donut Mob, etc.

For Bristol City away, February 1990, I travelled up with Paddy from Llanishen with whom I was friendly at the time. The train to Bristol was always a short and unpleasant trip, not helped obviously by the BTP who treat all football supporters like animals. Anyhow the long walk to Ashton Gate was always with incident and there were a number of minor scuffles outside various pubs on the way. I remember coming up to the turnstiles and there were some naughty, ugly looking Bristol who were looking for it but they were moved on by the police. The game as usual was tense and Bristol won the game 1-0 although the game was a very poor spectacle.

There was the usual hostile and intense atmosphere. As you would expect for a February evening, it was getting dark and there was light rain. Near the end of the game, I sat on a coach parked in the away area, Grays of Tredegar with Carter and Popeye from Llanishen were listening to the scores on the radio as it was raining. We then stepped off the coach as the game had finished and I stood next to it, talking to another few lads I knew, Wilburs and Ginger Simmo from Roath. We were about 15 or 20 yards away from the gate separating Cardiff from the Bristol supporters. At this point, we could see the large gate between the turnstiles being rocked back and forth by the Cardiff fans trying to get through to the Bristol and there were numerous items being thrown in both directions. There was a police van on the Bristol side, obviously filming (no CCTV in those days). It was at this stage that a few Cardiff lads climbed onto the turnstile roofs and began dismantling the roof and walls and throwing down the debris so that others could use it as missiles to throw at the police and Bristol supporters. This went on for about 10 minutes. There was absolute carnage and myself, Wilburs and Simmo saw all this leaning against a coach. When it all calmed down eventually and the home fans had gone, we were let out to make the long walk back to Temple Meads. I chatted to a few people I knew and was walking with another lad from Whitchurch and could see Temple Meads in the distance. With this, three Policeman come out of nowhere and jumped on me and pushed me against the wall. Not realising what I had done, they said I was being arrested for the turnstile incident and for hurling bricks, etc at the police and the Bristol fans. I denied all connection with the incident. This was at 5:15pm. I was taken to a station and placed in a cell until 11:20pm when I was eventually interviewed. I denied everything. I couldn't believe I was in this situation. The main incriminating factor was that I was wearing a Burberry Scarf!

I was eventually released at 1:00am. Now, everyone in those days had a Burberry scarf so it was not like I had a one-off Armani suit made especially for the occasion. The magistrates date was set and I used a local solicitor whom my mother knew. On the first day, I think about eight were up and the pleas went in. Four pleaded guilty including the lad on the roof from Gabalfa and four of us pleaded not guilty. Myself, Paddy from Llanishen, another lad and a young man called Anthony Rivers often known as Lakey (Soul Crew book author) whom I came to know pretty well. The four who pleaded guilty did not have to return until sentencing so it was just us four. I travelled to Court on most occasions with Paddy and his father. It was a journey we came to know well as I went eight times to the magistrates Court. Then a Crown Court date was set. The evidence from the Police on me was the fact I had this Burberry scarf. I had all statements, etc from the CPS and the police and these were very inconsistent. I also had a very poor video tape which contained footage from the police van on the other side of the fence. You could barely make out anything so what little evidence they had on me wasn't even helped with the footage. As I had said, it was getting dark on the day at the match and raining. According to the police statements, it was like a summer's day at lunchtime. The Crown Court hearing began and was set for two weeks. The Jury was sworn in and I said to my brief, I didn't want any Bristol City supporters on the case. I remember one lad put his hand up and had to leave the Jury. The Prosecution came first. At least ten of Avon and Somerset's finest gave their view of events which were totally incorrect, each saying again how good visibility was and how it was such a nice day. The sun was beating down, etc. This went on for nine days, each officer giving their view of events. It was flaky to say the least. After the 9th day I think it was, the Judge had obviously heard enough garbage coming and before we even had the chance to defend ourselves, the Judge called a halt and the four of us were let off. The four who pleaded guilty received six months each. To say I was relieved would be an understatement. To have spent all this time going over to Bristol a total of 17 times for no reason at all was a joke. However it was nice to get an apology from the police. That last bit was a joke. After this, my mother who had always held the Police in high esteem, was longer a supporter of them and has resented them since this episode.

After this episode, I stopped going down for a few months and played Saturday footy as it had put me off a bit. If you can go through this for doing nothing at all, what's it all about. However the lure of live football, friends and drinking soon had me back on the terraces and I still attend regularly home and away. Older and wiser I hope.

Chapter 17
Victory In Chesterfield
Gwyn Davies, CCFC

Chesterfield: not the first place that springs to mind when referring to a spot of bother at the footie is it? But it certainly nearly caught us out in March 2002. I was responsible at the start of that season (2001/2002) of putting together an 'organisation' known initially as the Valley Rams. My plan was to organise some regular transport to Cardiff away games based loosely around three of the larger Valleys leading off the City of Cardiff. The three Valleys in question were the Rhondda, Aberdare and Merthyr, hence Rams and also the play on our sheep shagger tag we get labelled with - this tag is chanted at us at every ground we visit and rather than upset us, we can usually be seen joining and dancing along to the sheep, sheep, sheep shaggers. It does confuse the locals somewhat as they seem to expect us to be destroyed and hold our heads in shame. Our initial aim as an organisation was to simply provide regular affordable coach travel which catered more for the 'laddish' type of fan, the type who liked a pint on the way there and also a pint on the way home. I was hoping and expecting to fill at least one bus full on a regular basis for our away trips. Up until now on a good day, each valley would have scores of lads at these games, all travelling under their own steam, vans, cars, trains and for some games, coaches. On the big games, each valley area could muster several coaches from their towns and villages. On some of the crap midweek games or boring other end of the country type games, you would have a regular level of die hard support but spread out over a large geographical area, making it hard for people to get together as a group. Part of our plan was to give all these people a central booking point and phone number and get them all together rather than in separate cars, etc.

Our first away game as the Valley Rams was to Peterborough United. The one proposed bus had turned into three and the next away game, it rose to five and so on. Actually within six months, we had drawn Spurs away in the League cup and finished up filling 32 coaches within a fortnight of the game being announced, a logistical nightmare. We had obviously carved a niche for our group and the more relaxed method of travel was appealing to vast numbers. In no time at all, we had to change the title from Valley Rams to the Cardiff and Valley Rams because so many lads from other Valleys and the City of Cardiff itself wanted to be a part of what we had started. The rest is history and there could be another chapter in this story at a later date (watch this space).

Anyway, back to the Chesterfield game. We had, as an organisation, been up and running just over six months. We were the most organised/disorganised gang/mob in the country. There were identity struggles. Some groups had ideas or visions of how they wanted things to run. We had extremes amongst us, bordering from some wanting it to be a total lads up for a bit of organised scrapping right the way down to others wanting another fully official organised supporters club with elected officers and a democracy in place. Well, this was my baby and democracy at these stages was 'this is what's happening, this is where we are heading, join in or fuck off and go and do your own thing'.

We would hold regular weekly meetings and take these around from town to town. Sometimes we'd have 300+ people turning up for a meeting. Mad, mad days but great fun. I had built up a small army of 'reps' as we called them. In most cases, these were the well known and respected lads from many areas; usually lads who had earned the respect by being able to have a scrap but also keep things organised for booking and controlling all the individual coaches. Finding scrappers wasn't the problem. It was the ones who could scrap and organise was the hard part but we got there.

The rivalry between the 'Valley Boys' and the 'City lads' was well known, culminating in the mid seventies with almost an all out war. Many times you'd see the look of bewilderment on away fans faces when they would be surrounded by police in the stadium for their own safety only to see massive scraps breaking out all over Ninian Park between rival factions of the home support. A scary old place, even for the home fans.

Well, this rivalry didn't just limit itself between Valleys and City or even Valley to Valley. I along with many others had grown up in a village where all the boys on my side of the street were enemies of the boys on the other side of the street but our united enemies which bound both sides of our street together were the next street in the same village and, my god, the next village down the road were the mortal enemies of our village. To pass through each other's villages, you either had to be mobbed up, tooled up (which at 10 was a catapult, 12 a big stick, 14 a club or cosh and 16+, a knife - I'm sure you get my drift, a bit of a growing up game that some time had dire consequences) or sneak through under cover of darkness. Occasionally for the big scraps, two or three villages would mob up and have a go at the townies. So basically what I'm trying to say is that the rivalry and tribalism was very much and still is to a lesser degree part of growing up in the Valleys especially where reputations and respect earned from previous battles was paramount. So getting all these boys to mix, meet and travel together wasn't always that straight forward. Often, I would get to a service station or pub, etc only to be called upon to try and sort out some situation. Sometimes I would have to give out an occasional slap just to keep some order and solve a problem. Thankfully that wasn't every week and it did get less and less as we progressed.

Chesterfield away was meant to be a chill trip; no history of real problems. Whilst it was known that they could always muster a tidy little mob, it was very much a case of minnows swimming amongst sharks. No-one was expecting problems; no battle plans in place and in fact, we were so complacent that we had booked a hotel in the town and 40 odd of us were staying for the night. We were taking around 12 or so Rams coaches up that day and the 40 odd that were staying were made up of small groups from several buses who would get off the coach they had travelled up on and all come home together on the one coach that was staying up there. Sounds easy but, believe me, another logistic nightmare.

It was my suggestion to make a night of it in Chesterfield; I had lived up there for a twelve months or so many years ago with work. The place was well known for nightlife and shed loads of tottie, a good mix for our travelling Rams. I was more than convinced we could have a good fun night without any running battles but I couldn't have been further from the truth. One of the attractions of travelling on a Rams coach was the drinking culture we fostered or rather harnessed because we at the Rams didn't invent drinking at football but we did identify early on that we could use the drink culture as a carrot if you like to get people on board in an organised group. Our plan from the early stage was to select fan-friendly pubs along the route or on the way home and, if possible, near the grounds we would be visiting. I would contact these in turn, trying my best to charm the landlords and assure them that I wouldn't be turning up with Genghis Khan's Mongol hordes. We would offer a bond of £200 and tell them that they could hold on to this money to cover any damages (which luckily there never was).

The older more respected heads amongst us made sure that the younger hotheads behaved and didn't mess up our drinking privileges. Anyone who stepped out of line wasn't banned but a couple of them were smacked or put in their place and simpled in front of their mates. This usually did the trick and often they would apologise (when sober) and get back on track or fuck off and do their own thing. Our reputation for keeping order and control amongst ourselves soon earned us notice not only amongst pubs the length and breadth of the country but also amongst some more forward thinking police forces, especially the West Midlands, NOT!

This progressed as far as publicans phoning me if they knew we were in the area and asking us to call in there with the guaranteed till bursting revenue we would bring along. Thinking back now, I should have been a bit more switched on and taken or asked for a few bungs. The police as I have said in some areas, realised the potential of keeping us together rather than having us spread out all over the county, travelling under all modes of transport and drinking in any pub that would either let us in or were too timid to stop us swarming over them. Many times we would be approached by the police asking us to set up either some pre-match meetings or emails, etc with them asking what they could do for us and us telling them what we could do for them. Sometimes they would promise us things, then stitch us up forgetting that we'd be back next year. They soon saw which option was the easier to manage but negotiating and even talking to this mob of hooligans (as we were and still are seen by many) went against the grain of some of the higher-ranked, public school educated, match Commanders.

One such incident was the first game at Wigan away. We had arranged with the police to take all our coaches to the JJB stadium. They had arranged a nearby pub for us all to go to, job done. Twelve coaches of Rams, straight to the ground, straight off the bus and straight into the pub, a good swig and into the game, the game ends, you come out and onto the coaches and head home.

Sounds simple and it can be but what they decided to do at Wigan was to let us all get into the ground and then turn up in ten van loads and search the coaches from top to bottom. Now one of the unwritten perks that we allowed the lads was that, for these long away trips of five hours on a coach, rather than stop on the way home for a drink etc, we'd allow them to keep a few cans in their bags as long as they were locked under the coach for the return journey. The drivers would then get ten or so miles on route, find somewhere safe to pull over and allow the lads to get their drink and have a safe trip home without the worry of stopping off in towns for drink and food and all the problems that would often cause. So, the police, on finding this stash of the dreaded alcohol, thought they'd solved the crime of the century. Bags were thrown onto the floor, some stamped on smashing MP3 players and the like and, in one case, a lad's Insulin and needles needed for his return journey.

Well, picture the scene at Wigan. I get to hear of this smart piece of police work and I then speak to our Police FIO who, in all fairness, is switched on and can see the broader picture but, at the end of the day, he is only a constable and there is only so much he can do. We both speak to the Match Commander who is proud of his great police work in finding some cans of alcohol stashed away for the homeward bound journey. I then point out to him that he will now need to block every exit on the way out of Wigan and on the route home because, as soon as these lads see a gap, they will be down there looking for refills or simply finding a pub to stay and drink in. It was funny to see the realisation of the situation occur to him. He was quite clear in stating the ways of the law to me in as much as the only place you could not drink on the way to football games was on such coaches. I replied, "No problem. So the 2,000 or so Cardiff fans you have safely wrapped up in stadium would still come next year but not in a recognisable largely compliant convoy of coaches but in scores of vans, mini buses, cars, etc and these will be parked all over Wigan and his officers will be running around like headless chickens trying to stop disorder." You could see the realisation and panic set in; suddenly you had a load of police vans bringing back these dozens and dozens of bags and dumping them outside the coaches. Many of these bags had been stamped on, many were just strewn around the coach park. How were they to know which bus they'd come off. Anyway it was sorted to some degree. Not everyone had their correct bag or correct amount of drink but at least the damage was limited. Next year came along and they took an almost grovelling approach with them offering the world to keep us on the coaches and sticking to the plans we had set up the year before.

Meanwhile, the areas that worked with us usually spoke highly of the cooperation and better behaviour they'd come across. However these areas would soon start moving the goal posts (and again a story for another day). Whilst initially they were happy to allow a few 'perks' and be pleased with the results, they would soon be limiting the perks and demanding even bigger and better results. Six years ago, they were happy if they had us out of town with no riots or major public disorder occurring. Soon they would be complaining about the amount of litter that 15 coaches would discharge and that some of the lads had even been drinking. Shame on them. Drinking on a day out at the football. Who did these hoodlums think they were?

Anyway, whilst every day didn't work out as we planned, most did and we were having a good time of it. The arrest figures that had kept us at the top of the disorder league of shame started to decline. Not only were we delivering a plan that worked but we were also giving them documented proof that it worked and that a little 'joint' enterprise would suit all parties.

The day of the Chesterfield game as I've stated was a bread and butter game to us. No expectation or real history of serious trouble and not expecting any. The police had promised to put us all in a pub near the ground and keep us together. When we were around two or so miles out of Chesterfield, I had the sense that things were a bit tense. Outrider motor bikes started picking up the coaches as they appeared. Nothing new there. We were taken to a large pub with a large car park. There were police everywhere but again, nothing new to us. Everyone was given a Sectioned 60 whilst getting off the bus and whilst not a new phenomenon, it did seem a bit over the top for a Chesterfield game. As happened at lots of other away games, the lads on the coaches would get calls from their mates. Some had made their way in cars and vans but they would still want to meet up with us; the atmosphere was guaranteed and there was also the safety in numbers approach at some of the more high profile games we encountered.

Again this was another bonus and spin off effect of what we were doing. By allowing a huge mob of us to stay together, this usually attracted a lot more Cardiff fans to come to the same pub or pubs as us and this would make policing us easier as long as they didn't wind us up too much. You may have had up to 1,000 people drinking in one or two pubs close to each other which makes a powerful mob if the need arose. It was also a massive deterrent to any hostile away fans who wanted a pop at us. My God, they couldn't have reached within a half mile of us and, if they did with the numbers we had, they'd have been slaughtered.

We started getting calls off small groups of Cardiff that had gone into the town centre. They had also said there was a huge police presence in town that day. I spoke to our FIO who couldn't say too much but it became clear later why they were all so tense. Chesterfield had amassed a huge mob for this one and we found out later from police sources and other lads that some major faces from several clubs in the area had grouped together for a 'United Yorkshire' v Cardiff confrontation. This was kept quiet from us and thank God because, whilst not looking for trouble, the majority of our lads would be straight in at the first chance of a ruck. That's just the way it is and I make no apologies for that. Leave them alone and treat them with respect and, in most cases, you'll get no problem but throw down a gauntlet and they'd be right up for it. If the word had got out whilst we had scores of coppers around the pub, they'd have needed a small army to keep these lads away from the town centre. They'd have run the two miles into town if they thought there was trouble brewing.

Anyway, we had our pre-match swig and were taken into the game. There were stories of minor offs taking place before the game. Sadly many scarfers and family groups were getting picked on and some had been slapped before the game. This had right wound up the lads and after the game, loads tried to break through the

111

police cordons around the coaches. There were a few minor arrests but no real disorder. Our group of 45 (the overnighters) stayed together and were lumped in with the couple of 100 lads who'd come up by train, for an escort back to the station and, in our case, the hotel at the bottom of town. It was like a military operation. Helicopters hovered above and every junction we passed had a cordon of vans and coppers sealing it tight. They took us a real long way around and did all they could to avoid taking us near the town centre where most of the 'Yorkshire United' mob had gathered.

When we approached the station, we said goodbye to the train lot and were then taken down to our hotel. All our bags, etc were collected from the bus and we booked in with no problem. One of the more senior coppers asked me what our plans were for the night and I said we would just go for a pint or two later and in small groups rather than fully mobbed up. He asked me to try and keep it to as late as possible before heading out of the hotel so as not to draw attention to ourselves and hopefully let the Chesterfield mob disperse. We were happy to do this; most of us wanted a bath or shower and forty winks before the forthcoming night on the town. We all planned to meet in the hotel bar around 7:00pm and shortly after this time most of us were in place.

We came to hear when we at the bar from four of the lads who had come back around the 6:30pm mark. These lads had not been with us at the game. They were all serving bans for previous trouble in the years passed. One had a five year ban and three of them had three year bans and were not allowed near the game. These four lads had had an afternoon pub-crawling around Chesterfield and had met no problems until after the game when the pub they happened to be in turned out to be the main Chesterfield pub. This had filled to the brim around 5:30pm with all the massed Yorkshire's finest who had spent the previous half an hour making the token attempts at getting to our escorted mob whilst in between attacking a few families who had parked their cars in the town centre.

This is one of the problems of being a Cardiff fan. We are all seen as fair game and any code of conduct goes out of the window when we are in town. Kicking some bloke up the arse when he's getting in the car with his wife and kids is seen as a major result for a wannabe lad. It is a bit of a two-edged sword. Some of the non-scene Cardiff fans hate the 'Soul Crew image or tag' our club carries but many times they have been glad to see 20 or 30 of our best come around a corner or into a pub just as they are about to be attacked by the local yobs from which ever town we are in. This was the case at Molineux when their Subway Army came down the hill wading into all the normals, men, women and children who they considered as fair game; that is until our lads came out and battered them senseless back up the hill. Even the more 'anti hooligan' Cardiff fans were cheering on the lads who scattered the Wolves lads all over the road and the banking outside Molineux.

Back to the four lads in the pub. Post match Chesterfield, they had managed to keep their heads down and blend in. Luckily there were so many strange faces amongst the Chesterfield mob that no-one really picked them out until one of the lads had to get a refill at the bar and didn't have enough sense to realise that "Oi, Butty, three bows and a lager when you're free," in a strong Welsh accent would attract just the slightest attention. It spread like wild fire. One of the lads was in the bog and just as he opened the door to return to the boys, he could see all the Chesterfield boys bouncing around the bar calling it on with the three remaining lads. He was weaving his way through when it went mental. Glasses, chairs, ashtrays, the full armoury was flying at the lads through the air. The police were outside and heard the commotion but, because of the packed nature and chaos in the pub with some people trying to get out and the coppers trying to get in, the three lads ended up trying to holding off the mob with chairs. Then, one lad was stuck in the middle of the Chesterfield lads thinking, "Oh fuck, how do I get out of here alive?"

Luckily as is the case when there is that many people trying to attack so few, they tend to get in each other's way and the lads, whilst in danger, did not take too many direct hits. Finally, the coppers forced their way in and escorted the lads out. By now, the floor was inches deep in smashed glass and there were tables and chairs all upended; absolute chaos. The four lads, now safely outside, were buzzing on adrenaline and giving it the big one now, taking the piss that even with those numbers they hadn't been battered but it was probably more the relief of getting out alive that had them buzzing.

They were taken in a van and dropped off at the hotel where they had great pleasure in each telling us their own version of events whilst slagging off the dopey twat who had ordered the drinks in the strongest Rhondda accent heard up north for a while. All this excitement was adding to the buzz going around the hotel bar. Whilst most of us thought the main event had taken place, a few of us still half expected a bit of afters, possibly a little later on and afters there would be a plenty.

Around the 7:45pm mark, I told the others to stay put whilst me, Dean and Bombers went up the hill to the first pub for a skulk around and to see how the land lay. The pub was a typical man's pub, 30 to 40 people in the bar, a couple of possible lads but nothing too naughty. No-one seemed to be staring or sussing us out. A few lads were on their mobiles but possibly being a bit naïve or not too paranoid, I didn't pay to much heed to this. We had one pint and then went back to the hotel. We said it looked 'ok' and we should head up there in dribs and drabs, have a pint and then see how it went from there. By now our motley crew had a few more numbers. Flahty, whose wife was a local, was staying up there with his in-laws and thank God he was because he's a great lad to have with you in a scrape. There was two or three others who lived around the Nottingham area who were also staying with us for a pint. All in all, besides the four Ferndale girls who had come with us (tottie on tour and anywhere for a night out and a great little gang), there were two old blokes who just made up the numbers which was Corky with his one leg and the other being the bus driver. We did have a good 35 or so lads who could be called upon if need be and soon enough they would be.

There were still a few small groups of lads in the pub but still no staring or eye contact. One or two did leave after few minutes of us getting in there and a couple of our more switched on lads started getting twitchy. Carlton, one of our lads, locked one of the two doors from inside saying, "If they are coming in, they are only coming in through one door." I was popping in and out and looking up and down the hill but not seeing anything out of the ordinary. I was now starting to relax. Back in the pub, I had just been served with a full pint when Ian shouts out, "Here they come." Everyone goes to the window but it's just eight or nine lads walking down the hill and heading for the pub. I just thought they were a group of locals out on the piss. They came in through the one open door. The lads let the first three in and then knocked the next two spark out with stools. I thought, 'fuck me, that's a bit heavy lads'. The ones who hadn't come in ran for their lives down the hill and the three that did get in took a few slaps and were allowed to run back out.

Then the shout went up, "Here they are." I looked up the hill and could see a good sized mob and they were being joined by more and more still coming around the corner at the top of the hill. Fuck me, everything was rushing through my head. I had brought everyone into this and I felt a massive responsibility. One of the lads chucked a stool through the pub window out onto the street. Perhaps it was a message to say bring it on, perhaps it was a plan to have one less window they could smash through onto us but, either way, the sound woke me up with a start. "Come on, outside all of us," I shouted. Everything was rushing through my head. We had a few options - stay in the pub and possibly getting trapped; fuck knows how many were coming down at us or outside where we'd have a chance to weigh it up. Also if it became too heavy, we could back our way down to the hotel. I started getting paranoid and thinking perhaps they have planned this well and if we backed off down the hill and what if they have another mob waiting in a side street at the bottom of the hill and we get stuck in the middle.

I'm also thinking that an hour or so ago, there were 300 coppers crawling around here. Surely they will soon get back when the shout goes up. Was I wrong with that one or what? I'm shouting at the top of my voice, rallying the troops and trying to make them think that I'm as hard as fuck even though my arse was twitching slightly. I'm shouting for everyone to stick with me, anyone run or take a backward step and they are dead. Sounds mad now and corny as fuck but this was quite scary and also as exciting as hell. Anyone who's had a taste will know what I mean. I was trying to size things up. It didn't look good. We were half way down a hill. They were on top coming down at us. There were 35 or so of us and what looked like 150+ of them and that's just the ones we could see. To make matters worse, they were at the top of the hill. Also at the top of this hill was a big fuck off skip with enough ammo to start a war. They were chucking everything at us, bottles were smashing around us, bricks bouncing off cars, bits of timber even tins of paint (more on that later). Any initiative they had, they didn't use fully. Instead of rushing down the hill and swamping us, they were only taking tentative steps forward and still chucking everything they could whilst we were getting right pissed off. Sensing their indifference to a full scale scrap, we started going up the hill at them. We spread across the road giving them an easier target for the missiles but it made us look like more of a threat. A couple of our lads had picked up some of the shit they'd thrown at us and were lobbing it back at them but it's a bit harder throwing up a hill.

As we approached the top of the hill, it now looked like a bomb site. We had been outside now for what seemed like ages but in reality could only have been a few minutes. Still no sign of the police. Let the battle commence. We were now face to face with their mob. They were giving it the big one, dancing around, no-one was stepping forward to have a pop. No problem there because we had plenty right up for it now especially the Rhondda boys who were annoyed at having their drinking session interrupted. Stick, the Rhondda rep. went straight into them followed by his brother who was one of the banned lads from the pub incident earlier. Two of theirs go down and none of their lads help them. They are still dancing around making all the noises and shouting all the threats. This was more to wind each other up and try and get a bit of bravery amongst them. Our lads on the other hand weren't doing much shouting but instead were picking out targets. I couldn't believe it. We were squaring up one on one all over the place and, other than the ones we were scrapping with, the rest of them were just looking at each other, hoping someone else would fill the breach.

All this just added fuel to our lad's tanks and they were now in full flow. There were quite a few lads sparked out or rolling around the floor. Out of the corner of my eye, I could see the four girls, the driver and the two old guys standing against a shop front as if watching a prize fight. No panic. They were chatting and smoking away as if this was an everyday occurrence. Mind you, in Ferndale it ain't far off the truth. I was making myself as visible as possible. At 6' 6" and 20 stone that ain't hard to do. It's always good to keep the big ones at the front and the little ones behind. Does make them think twice. As I was going up the hill, someone had thrown a mop or some sort of brush at me. It had a lime green luminous type handle. I had caught this in mid air and was now waving it over my head like a light sabre. Dean reckoned I looked like Darth Maul from Star Wars going up that hill waving this light sabre around. These Yorkshire lads must have thought we were extras in a film set and, if you seen some of ours, you'd understand where I'm coming from. Steven Spielberg would save a fortune on makeup if he made a film up here in the valleys.

Fuck me, where are the coppers? We must have been at it now for over ten minutes and that's one hell of a long time in a full scale scrap. At one time, I was going to ask for a timeout but didn't think it apt. One thing I'll never forget is seeing this one lad amongst us. I'd never seen him before but he stood out. He was well over six foot, quite skinny and he had a bandana around his head. He was like Bruce Lee. He was doing round house kicks and dropping people like flies. I found out later that he was from Chesterfield and a local in the pub we'd been in. He didn't even know there'd been a football game on. He just thought his local pub was under attack and he would help this gang of nice lads to defend it. Thank fuck he was on our side. Funny as hell but it all added to the night's madness.

Finally, I could hear sirens. Well at least one and that turned out to be an ambulance. Mad ain't it. At least someone had noticed there was a battle taking place on the main road through Chesterfield. Seconds later another siren and this time it was the police but it's only two coppers and one of them was a police woman. Fuck me, were they all on tea break or what? My God, let me tell you now. If you are going to rob a bank in Chesterfield, do it at 8:00pm on a Saturday

- you could have spent half the money before the police get there. As the coppers get out, they can see the seriousness of the situation. They are radioing for more help when the policewoman gets hit on the head with a bottle which has come over from the Chesterfield side. This galvanises our lads even more. Police or not, you don't hit women. The lads steam into the area where the bottle came from and the two coppers join in with us, battering all in front of us. My God, we had a proper little mob now. 35 Taffys, a Chesterfield Kung Fu pisshead and two coppers - Top Mob!

By now, you could see the Chesterfield lot losing numbers from the back of the mob. Several of their main lads were still shouting and trying to keep things together but you could tell they were well pissed off that we'd more than held our own. They would never get a better chance to turn us over or get a prized scalp. Our lads were high fiving it and hugging one another, comparing cuts and bruises and laughing. A lot of this was from relief at coming out of this scrape more or less in one piece. Next thing going through my head was, 'Oh fuck, CCTV' and who was going to get pulled. It's funny but I have been in some scrapes in the past and even though you are aware of cameras when such things happen, you just go for gold and then later when you calm down, you start to think 'oh fuck' and this was one of those moments. I had to plan a story. No, I wasn't smashing people over the head with this broom handle. I was just returning it to the nice man who'd thrown it down to me earlier and I was only rolling around on the floor with that lad because I thought he was having a fit and I was trying to save him from harming himself. "Honest Guv." You know the scenario.

Two ambulances had now turned up and seven or eight people were carted off to A&E. Luckily none of them were ours and apart from a few bruised hands and feet and a few cuts and scrapes, it was just like another day at the office for most of them. The police were now turning up in numbers and a bit embarrassed that they'd missed the action. It had taken place right under their noses and I should imagine a few awkward questions were to be asked about the post match policing and intelligence that day. There were no arrests made of our lads but I'm led to believe a few Chesterfield lads had early morning calls and quite a few were banned after the events of that night.

Later, I was relieved to find out that the lads who'd tried to get in the pub at the start of the night were some of theirs looking for it. They had planned to slope in and, when it kicked off, attack us from inside the pub as well as outside. A good plan but they come unstuck. Thank fuck a few of my lads were a bit more switched on and less trusting than me. We could have wound up with a totally different result.

Some of the police who had arrived by the dozen now that it was too late, then bubbled us up and escorted us down the hill to the hotel. In all fairness, they weren't too heavy with us. I think they could see from the numbers involved and from the story given by the female police officer that we were very much the attacked party who were just defending ourselves and taking care of business. Even so, when we arrived at the hotel, it was made clear to us that we would not be free to roam around Chesterfield again that night (or ever again if they could help it).

116

Mind you, half a dozen of the lads had soon formed an escape committee and within the hour, they'd somehow managed to get out the back way through a toilet window and then jumped into a taxi to have a night on the lash in Mansfield. The rest of us just settled down for the night in the hotel bar, recounting the story and answering the many mobile phone calls we were getting off all the lads on their homeward bound coaches. One or two of the coaches wanted to turn around and come straight back up for round two. It didn't matter that they were now 140 miles away from Chesterfield but our policy of never leaving a man down was proving true. Even though we never really had a man down that night, they all felt robbed of a good square up and if we had of played Chesterfield the following year, we'd have had enough volunteers to fill three hotels ('LoL').

I read in one of the local papers that the over dramatic hotel manageress had described the hotel like a hospital waiting room - silly cow. She was a right drama queen and was trying to find any excuse possible to throw us and our bags out on the street. Short of a few grazed knuckles and the odd shiner, the place looked more like a typical Valleys pub on a good night. The major damage that we'd taken was the 'Pink Paint'. None of us had noticed at the time but during all the commotion and missile salvos, some of the objects thrown were tins of pink paint that must have been in the skip. The next hour was spent seeing who had the most splashes over their shoes and clothes. Anyone found with splashes on their backs was accused of running away from the trouble even though in all fairness not one of them had taken a backward step. It was decided that all members of the night's fracas would from there on be honourable members of the 'Pink Paint Posse'. Later on, just for the crack, I had a load of business cards printed with the Pink Paint Posse logo and the letters '**V.C.**' printed in bold. This would now be known as the medal for Victory in Chesterfield. Seems a bit childish now but it all helped to bind these lads and all the others in our organisation even closer together. This was the first major test of a mixed Valleys bus and they'd passed with flying colours. There had been a lot of trust gained that night and people now knew that if it came on top, even if the lads you were with weren't from your town, you could still count on them as one of your own.

Just to put the icing on the cake, when we woke up the following morning, the same drama queen of a manageress was on duty and she was insisting that she was holding back the deposit that we'd given on a credit card when booking the room. She was insisting that this was to be kept back to cover the damages in some of the rooms we had booked. Well (keeping my fingers crossed and trusting the lads) I insisted that I accompany her around each of the rooms that we had booked. It gave me great pleasure to find every room in good order with not so much as a towel stolen or even a cup smashed. In fact, in some of the rooms the lads had even made up the beds (the soppy sods). Old habits and a smack off their mothers too many times in the past had served them well. One up for the Valley Rams and it was the first time that weekend that I'd seen the drama queen stuck for words. They may know how to fight but they also know how to behave when need be. A great bunch who in most cases I would trust with my life.

Chapter 18
"Don't mention the War"
Stefan
(Offenbach FC, Germany)

I met Stefan (Hofmeister) quite a few years ago and he told me all about the German hooligans. By this time, he already knew all about Cardiff and the Soul Crew. What he didn't realise was that the lads were so 'PASSIONATE' about their club and that, even though they liked the violent side, they followed Cardiff City like any other fan. The truth of the matter was that during the 80's and part of the 90's, the lads were 90% of Cardiff's away support and no matter how shit the team was, they were there, week in, week out. Stefan would tell me time and time again that without the lads, there would be no atmosphere .Stefan is now back living in Germany and I met up again with him last year in Frankfurt when Wales were playing there. I asked him if he would give an account of his days with Cardiff.
Annis.

Coming to Cardiff for the first time in April 1990, I had my first taste of what Cardiff City is all about: PASSION. I was born in Offenbach (Germany) and grew up on the terraces of Offenbach's Bieberer Berg Stadium. Visiting the Welsh capital as an 18 year old, I felt very much at home from the beginning. Cardiff in those days wasn't exactly a tourist resort just like Offenbach which still isn't. The local footie team had a tough time with difficulties on and off the pitch, either struggling not to get relegated or trying to bounce back – just like Offenbach.

On my way into Cardiff, I bumped into two City fans my age wearing football colours. Being absolutely footie-mad, I enquired about who's playing and in my naivety asked if I'd be able to purchase a ticket at the then unknown, Ninian Park. Yes I know... stupid question. Meeting my new friends at Ninian, watching a glorious 3-1 over Walsall, I soon had the 'being home' feeling. A traditional football ground, extremely passionate supporters and a team, I felt I could (with a bit of training) play for myself. Anyway, I was hooked. Dunno if it was the masochist in me but I followed the Bluebirds from that day and I never regretted it. I was always different in that most of my childhood and teenage friends were glory hunters. Bayern Munich could win the league twenty times in a row but I still wouldn't follow them. My local side Offenbach who were down to the 4th league for some time, always saw me cheering them on. Same goes for Schalke 04, the team my Dad and Grandad always followed. Being a good son, I followed

119

the family tradition and had a soft spot for the 'Knappen'. I remember the kids at school laughing at me because Schalke then were at the bottom of the 2nd league and Offenbach in the 3rd.

Who cares?

It was tough though to keep up with the Cardiff scores as the internet wasn't as common those days and the German sports magazines never focused on English lower league football. So I bought English newspapers and English mags like 'Shoot' or 'Match'. This of course changed with the World Wide Web and my interest in Cardiff City would start to bloom properly. From now on, I'd try to watch City during my holiday trips to Britain, mostly away matches as I have good friends living in Sussex and Glasgow (where I watched Celtic too). On one of those trips, a friend and I managed to get a ticket for City's Friday night away trip to QPR in the 2002/2003 'Millennium Season'. Arriving in central London that afternoon was a kind of taste what to expect later that evening. In the tube, in the stations and the inside of pubs, we saw football lads from different London firms. All, we soon would find out, on their way to Loftus Road; their aim to have a 'look' at Cardiff's travelling contingent.

Wearing no club colours or badges, we managed to get to Shepherd's Bush without any problems. Again the tube was full with lads (those I am sure were Millwall). It was an 'everyone against the Welsh' event where the Londoners would put local rivalries aside to put those Taffys in their place. By the time we arrived, the whole place had been invaded and taken over by Cardiff fans who took the micky out of their English counterparts. Walking on the streets, drinking, abusing and singing anti-English songs, chants of what to do with Royal family and disorderly behaviour with no-one being able to stop those Taffys. There were thousands of them, hardly any with football tops but loads of designer labels like Stone Island, Burberry... or, how they'd say in Jack land, 'Paraaada'.

A top night. City, actually it was Earnie, destroyed QPR 4-0. It was great watching the little man scoring a hat trick and Cardiff taking over the place. I witnessed minor incidents outside but my feeling was that the Londoners didn't stand a chance against a powerful South Wales force who were up and ready to fight. Cardiff were untouchable that night. Until then, I had never seen a firm of its size and strength like the Soul Crew that night at Shepherd's Bush. This was an international firm, big numbers but not organised. At this point, I should mention, I was and never will be a friend of stories or books where football lads tell fairytales and write they've never been done or their town firm is by far the best in the country, etc. Every firm, no matter how big and strong, has been done. Same goes for Cardiff only that, personally, I haven't witnessed an incident where someone defeated the Soul Crew.

I moved to South Wales the following season. Being a web and graphic designer, I accepted a position in the Welsh Capital and was from now on able to follow my team, week in week out for the next few years. Through my new contacts with the RAMS (a supporters group who organised away travels), I was put in touch with Annis Abraham and met him on several away trips. We've had good chats about football, especially about the City. He is CCFC mad like myself, only that he's been there a long time before me and of course always was and still is much closer and informed about what happens inside our beloved club. It was actually Annis, who nicknamed me 'Hofmeister' (well... still better than 'Schweinsteiger') and whenever I come to Cardiff, we meet up for lunch and watch the games at Ninian from Block A of the Grandstand.

A funny anecdote happened when I spent Christmas with my family. We were at my parents' house when my mother called me to tell me there was a documentary about Cardiff City on the TV. You can guess what they had on and when they showed some of those Cardiff nutters, my mum was in disbelief. When I told her that quite a few of them were my mates...

One of the most talked about incidents in the last few years happened at Molineaux when City defeated Wolves 3-2 in 2004. Our club had just sold Earnie to West Brom and we were in the relegation zone when my favourite player Graham Kavanagh scored our winner. A strong away support with almost 3,000 Cardiff fans made the trip to Wolverhampton. Still inside the stadium, we were overjoyed with the three points. News quickly made rounds that Wolves were outside trying to get a piece of Cardiff's reputation.

When I came out, a battle was already on. Wolves running down to meet Cardiff and our lot into their direction. It was a short but heavy encounter with Cardiff actually battering their Wolves opponents. Actually it looked more like fathers smacking their teenage sons teaching them a lesson, due to the age difference of the two mobs. The police soon became involved, trying to separate the two but it backfired as the now in rage Cardiff fans had switched their combat mode from stand-by to battle. A police car was wrecked; luckily no policemen were inside and Cardiff were in running battles with the West Midlands police. The situation calmed down and everybody made their way back to their coaches. The whole escalation of violence could have been prevented if the police would have kept the Cardiff following inside the ground until the Wolves boys had left or should I say, had their own ruck with the WMP. This failure caused another incident at Wolves the following season...

Arriving at Wolves, our CD player played "I predict a riot" which caused laughs as we were looking at an army of coppers outside. Brilliant timing, we were stunned by the large amount of officers dressed in combat gear, waiting for us. The atmosphere was aggressive. On the whole walk from the coach park down to Molineaux, there was a line of coppers with helmets, batons, shields and dogs on both sides. A dog almost bit me as I walked past it. I heard that others actually were bitten but I didn't see it. I watched the game from the Main stand that day, meeting an old friend from Germany who had wrote an article about Wolves. That's why I cannot comment on what happened inside the away stand at half-time but I saw riot police steaming from pitch side into the away section and quickly hitting out at anyone standing near the aisles. I heard that it kicked off properly inside but again, didn't see it.

I left the ground with two minutes to play. I expected the WMP to lock the away fans in and guard them to the coaches afterwards. My plan was to be out before anyone else so I'd be able to walk to the coach quickly and not having loads of coppers pushing me all the way up to the coach park. How little did I know. By the time I walked around the stadium, Cardiff were allowed to leave at the same time as anybody else. As soon as the last City fan left the stadium, riot police started to push and provoke the away followers. There were people (Wolves and Cardiff fans) queuing at a Burger van who, all of the sudden, felt a baton and were under attack. Although our fans were not in a fighting mood first, it led to Cardiff fans turning on the police and after several fans (including myself) were hit and a guy with crutches was hit on the ground, Cardiff fought back and hit out on every copper they could get.

All the way back to the coaches, Cardiff battled with the WMP, leaving quite a few Cardiff fans with open head wounds and two officers taken to hospital. I remember a documentary that I saw called the 'Battle of the Beanfield' when armed coppers hit out on a peace convoy full with hippies. I soon felt like one of those travellers. I didn't do anything but was left unable to defend myself against a brutal attack carried out by those who claim to represent the law.

Cardiff's reputation went sky high afterwards amongst football lads. Amongst shirts and scarfers of other clubs, it was a treatment that certain police officers thought that us Cardiff fans deserved, because we're animals... and Welsh anyhow.

A completely different experience was the League Cup tie at Bournemouth. A Tuesday night game, a small away following, not even a handful of coaches with almost 90% Cardiff shirts and families, hardly any football thugs amongst them. Being given a pub about ten minutes walk away from the ground, we found ourselves amongst friendly and talkative Bournemouth supporters who mixed with us in search of a pint. The atmosphere was relaxed as we never had any hassle at Bournemouth and the locals were friendly. But soon the peace was disturbed when a couple of lads in designer gear entered the pub looking around. We all asked ourselves who they were, were they newbies or even Bournemouth boys although they are not known to have dressers? Someone said they might be Valley lads that no-one had met so far. One Cardiff fan stepped up and asked them where they were from and the answer was

"We're West 'am and we're looking for Cardiff..."
"Well, you just found them, mate."
A battle cry went up.
"Kiaaardiff..."

It kicked off big time and for about 30 seconds everything came flying; glasses, bottles, chairs, tables. Everybody hitting somebody, in this chaos even Cardiff shirts joined in. As the probably 15 or so Cardiff lads dragged their attackers outside, they found even more Londoners waiting. There must have been around 50 of them, all ready and geared up to fight and about to steam into Cardiff. But those 15 Cardiff were some of the best lads I have come across and instead of taking the expected step back to find shelter in the pub, they just stood their ground and tried to defend themselves. They instantly took the initiative and attacked West Ham. Those 15 against 50 was an uneven battle and those Londoners weren't exactly inexperienced or shy to exchange greetings. One Cardiff fan was battered. I think he was hit by a brick and hit the pavement with his face, looked nasty anyhow. It was pretty even stevens. Later I heard some West Ham claimed they'd 'done' the Soul Crew that night. Well, if you were there, you'd say differently. Those 15 actually had a good go at West Ham and were anything but 'done'. They even managed to run some of their attackers who came back afterwards. But if you claim a glorious result attacking 15 when you have 50 and manage not to get smashed yourself... Well then, yeah, you have a story you can tell your kids about one day.

Police arrived pretty soon but, as it was clear who attacked who, no Cardiff fans were arrested. South Wales police officer Simon Insole should be mentioned here. I have met Simon on several occasions, a true gentleman with a great sense of humour and the most respectable policemen I have come across. If they all would be like him, I am sure you'd hardly have hassle at games. Fair and open minded, not that he wouldn't nick anyone who's crossing the line but he is fair and treats everyone with respect and doesn't try to stitch up anyone. Looking back at Bournemouth that night, he's pretty game as well. When West Ham attacked, he drew his baton and joined in as if he wanted to say "I am Cardiff, too...and these are MY lads". Dunno who 'awarded' him the tiny 'Cardiff on Tour' badge (which he still wears at games), but he is certainly one of us; a 100% Cardiff fan!

Over the years, he earned a lot of respect from everyone and although he's nicknamed 'Potato head', you will hardly find any Cardiff fans, young and old, who speak badly about him. And when you read these lines Simon (which I know you will be), keep up the good work but remember: ze sekret Gjermann police is votching you...

When we played West Ham away, it kicked off on our way into London. Some had attacked the coach convoy and all vehicles stopped and the doors came flying open, chasing the Londoners who geared up and found fierce looking weapons to hold those rioting Welsh hordes back by looting a fruit market! You can imagine the faces when apples and oranges came flying as missiles. I thought you only get that treatment in Italy. Now I know how Italian footballers feel when they come home from an unsuccessful international tournament with their national team. ICF... could it be 'I Chuck Fruits'? Love their club anthem? It goes 'I was throwin' apples, throwin' apples in the air...'

In late 2005, Cardiff were up at Hull. There is a certain history between the two clubs so everyone expected a rough welcoming at the East Coast. In the weeks prior to the game, some Hull made comments about Cardiff on the web, creating a bad atmosphere and the temper spoiled over amongst our travellers. Arriving at the KC, Cardiff fans started hurling abuse towards Hull and the police while entering the stadium. The game itself didn't help to improve relationships and the atmosphere was tense. With Hull pretty close to our end and some of the chants were just a little bit too much, some Cardiff walked over the netting entering the no-mans land by pushing stewards aside. Ready to get to Hull but, instead of Hull fans trying to do the same, they took a few steps back and police came instead to stop our lads and to restore the peace.

Towards the end of the game, a big mob of Cardiff tried to get into the no-mans land again to have a pop at Hull but with no success. The Old Bill were up and ready and everyone left the KC quickly. Outside, a steel fence with coppers on both sides was in place to prevent rival fans getting to each other. Cardiff started hurling missiles, hoping that it would cause a reaction by Hull. Again unsuccessful. Cardiff turned on the police who now tried to protect the steel fence which was about to come down as Cardiff fans clung onto it until they had pulled and pushed it down. Only after the police put the dogs in and officers on horses who were galloping along the fence, did our lot stop. Hull were nowhere to be seen. Even when all the coppers were on our side of the fence, not one Hull fan tried to come close to us.

It took about 45 minutes to get everyone onto their coaches. One super-dooper Hull copper didn't help by announcing that the coaches were due to leave in two minutes and whoever isn't on board by then, they'd be left behind. The coaches were empty again within seconds - that was an own goal, mate.

When we finally boarded the coaches and were leaving the coach park, everyone expected Hull to make a last attempt. They can't let us behave like nutters in their own town; we had been taking the piss. We were sure they would be ambushing the coaches when we drove through the park surrounding the KC. Excited and anxiously waiting for the events to come, hardly anyone sat down. It was still battle stations! But where were Hull? Not one brick (not even a stone) thrown at a coach, not one Hull fan was to be seen. I know that Hull have had a good reputation on their day and it is obvious that everyone respects Hull but that afternoon was a complete no show.

Many have asked me over the years, if it's true that Cardiff can pull large numbers, that the Soul Crew is one of the largest firms around and that they doubt reports of 1,000 and more Cardiff lads coming together for a game. Well, my friends, it is true. Cardiff on a good day IS the biggest firm I have ever seen. I'm not lying to you. There are thousands but not at every game and you don't get them all at the same place at the same time. I haven't met many football fans who are as passionate as Cardiff supporters but it's needless to mention that their firm isn't organised which of course is pretty hard due to its size.

There are separate groups from within Cardiff itself. Merthyr, Barry, the Valleys and even one small group originate from Newport and Chepstow. Some of these firms don't get on with each other only City unites them for a short time. People get older, wiser and lazier. Nowadays many can't be bothered anymore to leave a pint alone just to say 'Hello' to a rival supporter. Besides that, Cardiff certainly doesn't need to work on its reputation. They don't need to attract attention. There's already enough of that. They most just wait for the events to come to them and hardly anyone goes out looking for trouble.

I have made some great friends over the years watching the Bluebirds. Not only Cardiff supporters but also many Wrexham, Brighton, Millwall and even Leeds lads. What we all have in common is the love and passion for our football team. I never regretted the step to move to South Wales and while you get your ups and downs in your life or your job, following Cardiff City was certainly some of the best moments in my time living in the Welsh Capital. Being with your mates, travelling to watch your team play is my kind of favourite Saturday afternoon. I just love the whole experience, the pre-match pint, the laughter, the banter and the atmosphere especially when we are in good voice. While the Bluebirds are flying high and made it to Wembley, it has become a little quieter over the last two seasons but the passion for our club is still there. The scene has changed over the years just like we all change ourselves but don't anyone ever say the lads of Cardiff aren't true fans because I've seen from the outside their blood runs blue. The only thing that will never change is the love to our beloved Cardiff City FC. And that's for sure in my book, once a Bluebird, always a Bluebird.

Stefan (aka "Hofmeister" or "German Shepherd")

Chapter 19
The Jacks At The Exchange
John Simmonds (Simmo), CCFC

I have known Annis for years and he asked me if I would write the following chapter. I am known to everyone as Simmo (John Simmonds aged 52) and I have been a regular known face at Cardiff City for years. I'm not going to tell all the old war stories that other lads have written in this book, I was there for some but not all. The one thing that sticks in my throat is the total shit that was written in the Jack book about the night in September 2003 when they came down to my local, The Exchange in Canton and I am glad that Annis has given me the chance to set the record straight.

It was a Saturday night in September 2003. We had played Forest home that afternoon and the Jacks were meant to be playing at Mansfield which was later to be postponed. On the Friday night, the Exchange had over 150 lads out expecting Forest to come down as we had heard a whisper but as usual it was a lot of crap. On the Saturday afternoon just alone in Canton, we had well over 400 lads out for Forest but nothing happened that day. We started to hear the whispers again and this time that the Jacks were meant to be stopping off on their way back from Mansfield. Over the last 30 years, we must have heard it over a 1,000 times. That evening up until about 8:00pm, we still had nearly 200 lads in the Exchange because we knew the Jacks match had been called off. If they were going to come, they would have by now. So over the next hour or so, most lads drifted into town or headed home.

By 9:00pm, my local was virtually empty of lads and it was starting to fill up with some locals and few of the ladies from the bingo next door. At approximately 9:30pm a group of about 15 lads marched in. I looked at them and went straight over and said, "Are you Forest or you on a stag do lads?" With that this Jack bastard said, "Come on, we're Jacks." The next thing, bottles and glasses were flying back and forth. For the record, we had no more than seven lads including some local lads. We managed to group together and force them back out of the pub and at no stage did my son or I get punched by any Jack. At the door, we managed to hold them and with that, one of the Jacks was smashing our windows through. One of our lads just burst out the doors with a chair and ran into them and with that, we steamed towards them. In the street, there must have been over 25 of them and less than four of them stood. Of those, some of them took a pasting while their fellow Jacks just stood and watched from a distance. By this time, the Old Bill had arrived and whacked some of the lads that were with me. We had chased them as far as the old St David's Hospital which is well over 300 yards away. By now, the Jacks had virtually disappeared. I followed them around the corner where I saw them piling into their two mini buses. Two of us walked over and just laughed at them and with that the Old Bill sent us back.

What we can't understand is that the Jacks somehow think they had a victory. Yes, one of them was nicked for smashing a window but me and my son and one of my mates were dawn raided for it and not one other Jack was nicked for fighting.

I've seen the CCTV footage and the Jacks had gone and come back three times before they decided to enter the pub so they knew how few lads we had in there before they made their 'big' entrance. The real fact is there were more 'bingo' ladies in the pub than lads but maybe that's why they came in and as we all know the CCTV doesn't lie. It shows seven Cardiff and one chair chasing twenty five Jacks. Ha, Ha, YOU JACK BASTARDS !!!!!

Fan taken to away game

John Simmons: A Cardiff City fan who is well-known in the pubs around Canton.

The programme, which claims to show him goading rival fans in Wrexham, says "Simmo" was one of the fans taken to a game at Mansfield Town by club owner Sam Hammam.

Chapter 20
Fright Heart Lane
Chelsea Pat

When the draw came out of the hat, my phone literally blew up. Cardiff must have the only firm in Britain to get better and BIGGER as time goes on. They now have a bigger firm than they did in the 70's and 80's. Alternatively, it also could be that over time everyone else's mob became smaller and they stayed the same. Their team was shit so they seldom played the big boys and tales of their continued huge numbers was all second and third hand stories. Some stories though are based on fact as I had discovered a year earlier.

Tottenham were arguably one of the best firms in the country so it was a proper clash of the heavyweights. The weekend before the game, the Yids were playing Boro in the cup while Chelsea, my team, had West Ham. After the game, we were about 200 handed outside our pub listening to our mates from Boro as they taught Spurs a lesson on the Seven Sisters Road (the noise in the background was unbelievable). The action was being beamed live from a mobile phone. Judging by this, I didn't fancy Spurs chances on the Wednesday considering Cardiff would have at least 1,000 boys. However fate is not without a sense of humour!

A train strike on the Wednesday fucked up the trains so Cardiff had to make their way down in coaches and mini buses. They provisionally arranged to meet in Enfield and me and Bully from Chelsea, Ronald and Kray arranged to meet them. However when we arrived, there was a pub on our left and outside was a 6'2" black geezer with dreadlocks and a black Stone Island hooded jacket. He smiled at us revealing more fucking gold teeth than me. Sometimes you get a feeling that this is not going to be our day. This fucker then went back into the pub. "We've been sussed," said Bully. "Just keep walking," I said as we quickened the pace glancing back every few seconds. We stopped in the next pub to catch our breath. "Fuck me, that was close," Bully said. "What's the matter with you? You look like you've seen a ghost," he said. "I hope you've written a will, Bully cause we're fucking dead," I said. "Look over your shoulder but don't make it obvious." As Bully glanced back, 30 Yid youth waded into the bar with a 'football factory' swagger and ordered drinks. "Drink up," I said to Bully. "Nah, take your time. They ain't sussed us," said Bully. "Bully, I'll fucking kill ya if that Rasta walks in here and clocks us. They will dissect us." "All right mate, you're right." said Bully. "Let's fuck off."

Anyway fast forward two hours and we meet Annis at a petrol station where we jumped in a mini bus with some of Annis's mates. As we approached the ground, I noticed we were coming towards the home end. Normally when Chelsea play (unless we've done a sneaky one), we come from the other side of the ground. As we crawled through the traffic, we became caught in a jam. The next thing, hundreds and hundreds of lads came running down the road towards us both on the pavement and in the road through the traffic. "Oh my god," I hear a Welsh accent from the back of the van. "I take it that this lot ain't yours then," I asked. "Nope," said the voice. "Right," I said, "Nobody say nothing, I'll do the talking." As the pursuing mob gather around the van, their charge has now gone from a jog to a walk. As they get level with the van, all eyes and heads faced our way. All of a sudden, the driver door gets pulled open from the outside, loads of hate filled faces crowded around the open door, "Come on you, Welsh cunts," said a big skinhead in a CP Company jacket. "What you fucking on about?" I said, "We're fucking Yids, the row's back down there. Call yourself Tottenham. Why you going this way?" "Oh shit, sorry mate. We thought you were Taffys." "Yeah, do I fucking sound Welsh, you mug?" and with that I pulled the door shut.

Nobody said a word until we drove through the hundreds of them and we had reached the away end. I will never forget as we stopped, I looked back and everyone was as white as a ghost. "Anyone got a dust pan and brush," said the driver. "Why?" I said. "Cos I think I've shit all over the seat." With that, we all cracked up laughing; what a fucking escape. I had visions of them squaddies caught in the IRA funeral with Northern Ireland in the 80's and it definitely would have been if one of them had recognised me. Luckily the van had no name on it either.

During the game, the stories were coming back of Cardiff being picked off in small mobs as they made their way to the ground. To be honest, I wasn't surprised. As much as I hate the Yid cunts, the mob they had out that night was top draw. They would have done anyone that night and after what had happened the previous Saturday against Boro, even more credit to them to pull a mob like that.

In the stadium, Cardiff had at least 1,000 lads but, because of the train strike they were all over the place. If the train strike hadn't been on, I reckon there would have been total carnage and it would have been very hard to say who would have come out on top. After the game, the Yids tried to hold us back but Cardiff burst through the gates. You could see groups of Tottenham hanging around everywhere. We crossed the road. Cardiff steamed towards one group of Tottenham and battles commenced everywhere. After about five minutes of running battles, it calmed down but, to my horror when we reached the next corner, all the Cardiff lot turned right towards the White Hart Lane train station where all their coaches were parked. I had to go left towards Seven Sisters and I had lost Bully and Ronald. I was on my Jack Jones. Fuck me, I thought I'll never reach home. I must have been pulled at least three times by groups of Yids on the main road.

"Got the time mate?" "I'm Spurs" "Oh, sorry mate."
"Where you from mate?" "Tottenham" "Sorry mate."
"Where you from, you Cardiff cunt?" "I'm a Yid, mate." "Sorry mate."

I called this a St Peter movement. When he denied knowing Jesus, I denied being Cardiff, three times, ha, ha. Honestly, over the years, that was one of the dodgiest nights for me personally. When I next met Annis, we were laughing our hearts off about it. I was later told by some Cardiff that as they were marched down the road, there was a tennis Court by a park and about 30 Cardiff burst the escort to run through the Court into the park. Unfortunately, they were met by 400 Yids coming towards them, bad move. The rest of the Cardiff escort battled with the Old Bill to try to reach their mates but were battened back. However, a large mob of Cardiff had managed to sneak out and ran some mobs of Yids right by the park; the trouble was they were running into the middle of nowhere and became split into smaller and smaller groups and eventually were picked off again.

Not a good night for the Soul Crew but sometimes circumstances (the train strike) dictate the outcome rather than the strength of the actual mobs.

Chapter 21
48 Hours Notice To Meet One Of Scotland's Finest
Ian Thomas, CCFC

I am from the Rhondda which is in the valleys of South Wales. I have been a City fan all my life and have been going down Ninian Park since 1989 and watching us away since the double winning season of 1992/3. Being brought up as a City fan and following them for many years, you start to learn about things which happen off the field and being a City fan, this kind of thing tended to happen on a more regular basis than at other clubs. Over the years, I have come to know people who were well known in the casual culture. After my first experience of trouble with the City, I was hooked. When the pre-season fixtures were announced for the forthcoming 2004 season, we had the usual features close to home and lower league teams. Mansfield was on that list. City fans had been there so many times before and nothing virtually ever happened there apart from the odd skirmish so most City fans booked their holidays or if they weren't doing their summer holidays, then their Missus' would be filing for a divorce. Mansfield decided to cancel the fixture due to them not being able to afford the police bill. What were the police expecting? Cardiff to go in a big mob and start smashing the town to bits in a pre-season friendly. Come on, there would have only been a small crowd because Cardiff aren't exactly a big attraction as we were only in the championship.

So that's it. Another friendly cancelled due to the police bill; the second time in two pre-seasons. I didn't really mind because now I could go out on the piss all weekend instead. Then I had a phone call late on a Wednesday night saying that City had planned a friendly away for that same day. I wasn't really that bothered as I had made plans for the weekend until the next day when I found out that it was at Hibs. After my last visit to Scotland in another pre-season friendly at Motherwell, I saw first hand that the Jocks seemed well up for it. With just 48 hours notice to get the lads together, it was going to be hard. We thought there would only be a handful of us going but my mate Matthew phoned me up out of the blue and said there was a coach going. He booked me and another mate Tiny on; the rest of the boys that I know weren't that interested. After the initial buzz and excitement, I went for a couple of quiet pints at my local thinking about the day ahead. I obviously knew of the Hibs mob as they had a very good reputation and it would be interesting to see if they lived up to it. The Hibs mob were probably rubbing their hands together. Cardiff at home for a big firm like them; it was probably like all their Christmas's had come at once. But due to the lack of time we had to organise everything and I knew there would be a battle on our hands.

I didn't manage to get any sleep the night before so I was awake watching telly then I heard Tiny come bouncing down the road. We managed to convince one of the boys to drop us down to Nantgarw around 3:00am. We arrived there as the bus was pulling in. There was a few of the lads on it already. Another stop just outside Cardiff is where we picked up the rest of the boys and we were on our way. Me and the boys are used to long away trips, Hartlepool and Carlisle to name but a few. Me and Matthew had been on these trips many times before but this was the first time we had gone to Scotland by coach. We knew this was going to be a long old trip. Let's face it, everywhere is far from South Wales. Before it had even started to get light outside, the beer was flowing on the bus. It was going to be a long day; I decided to pace myself. After only a couple of hours, the toilet was starting to overflow. This bus was an antique from the second world war so a pit stop at the services was in order for the driver to empty the bog and have a quick fag and food stop and then we were on our way again. A couple of more pit stops up the motorway and we were coming into Scotland. We arrived at Edinburgh around midday and into Hibs territory a short while later.

Getting off the bus, a few of the lads went up the road and we followed them to the nearest pub. After being refused entry, we headed down this alleyway to a pub on the corner opposite a church, right by Easter Road. The pub was a shithole. Even the doormen were wearing Stone Island so we knew this was a home pub. I was walking around the place singing 'Hearts' songs as I am a closet Jambo which got me a few funny looks. Darryl had a call from Tex saying he and 25 others were coming down to meet us at the pub. There was around 20 of us here already and with only 48 hours notice there was a good mob of around 45/50 of us. With Hibs reputation, we knew we needed as many lads as we could get. All the boys were now inside the pub and it was a good mob with a few top faces there. We knew that if they decided to come and find us, we would be able to give them a good run for their money.

After a couple of hours in the pub and waiting to see if Hibs were coming to have a pop, a few of us decided to go and have a look outside and have a wander to see if anyone was having a mill around. There was a meat wagon with only a handful of coppers in it. A few of the boys had had enough of waiting around. They thought that nothing was going to happen so headed into the ground early. How wrong were they. Literally within minutes, there was a group of a good 50/60 Hibs and they were walking up the road towards us. I noticed that there was a good mix of older and younger lads in their group. Me and Matthew looked at each other and said 'here we go'. Vince came running out and the Jocks were now bouncing in front of us. For some strange reason, only around 10/15 Hibs came across to us with the rest of their lads just standing over the road looking at the situation and watching to see what happened.

What we didn't realise at the time was that the pub doors had now been locked behind Vince. By now there was only 6 of us. Vince doesn't waste any time. He just ran straight into the middle of them and smacked this one Jock clean out. Then a couple of Hibs went into Vince from the side. Me and Matthew smacked the pair of them clean out. Then all hell broke loose. I had a half drunk bottle in my hand and, due to being outnumbered, I smacked it into the face of one of them. He went down and blood was pouring from him. Next thing I knew, I was getting battered by five or six of them. The rest of our small group then steamed straight in. At one stage, we managed to back them off then suddenly a roar from across the road went up and the rest of the Hibs came flying over. A lad from North Wales who was with us ran up to this guy who looked like Giant Haystacks and knocked him out in one punch. A lad from Merthyr came and stood next to us and the six of us were now stood together. We were throwing punches but suddenly an avalanche of punches were being thrown back at us and I knew we were now going to get hammered.

The next thing, the lads in the pub behind us have kicked the fire exit through and steamed out in good numbers. Now there was around 35/40 of us. The rest of the Hibs had come steaming in. Credit where credit was due, they stood there until they couldn't take anymore. There were lads on the floor all around us but they showed some bottle. Even though we were completely on top, they never once left any of their mates behind and they were dragging them out even when they were getting a leathering. That was one of the main reasons, I have a lot of respect for their mob. Even though they were getting a battering, they tried all they could to help their mates that were down whereas a lot of other firms that I have witnessed would have done a runner.

Anyway, the police now decided to come steaming in after the reinforcements had arrived and, in a way, luckily they did. When Hibs were getting pushed back up the road, one had come up behind Vince and was about to stab him until one of the coppers intercepted him and knocked the blade out of his hand. The copper received a few slaps from the Hibs lads for his troubles. Then there was a calm. The police were now on top and had us all lined up against the walls outside the pub with cameras in our faces. Suddenly, we hear this massive roar to the right of us and there's well over 100 or so Hibs running down the road at us. Fair play, they looked well up for it. We all tried to turn around and advance towards them and likewise them to us. The police went mental and managed to keep us separated. Me and Matthew said to each other that if the 60-odd original Hibs had waited another five minutes, they would have had a much stronger and bigger mob and would have completely battered us. To us, in many ways, we had had a good result due to Hibs reputation. On the other hand, we'd had a lucky escape. If they had been organised, they would have had a very good scalp on their hands.

We were marched to the ground where me, Matthew and Tiny went in and only paid a quid. We watched as the older lads with us tried but they didn't manage to be so lucky. We walked up into the stands to watch the match. The ground looked decent due to redevelopments in recent years. Apart from an old single tier stand to our right which looked like where their lads were sitting and, fair play to them, they were bouncing around with a few trying to get into our end by running across the pitch. To save face, a few of us ran down the rows of empty seats to meet them. We only had around 120/160 fans who had made the journey due to the short notice of the match.

The game was now a non-event. Apart from yet another great goal from Earnshaw, there was really little else to shout about. During half-time, a Hearts fan came up to us and talked to us about what he had seen happen before the game. He said he had seen it all and said that we had given a good account of ourselves and he was glad to see a few of his arch enemies getting a battering. After the game, the police were on top. They held us in the ground for a short while and then escorted some of the boys who had come by train and car. We were put straight back onto our coach.

A long trip back to Wales was now the only thing we had left to look forward to. The bus was still buzzing and everyone was talking about what had happened. After a short stop in Bigger for refuelling and a restock on supplies, we were on our way again. After a power-nap on the way back, I woke to find Vince going through my bag helping himself to my cans. We arrived back at around 2:00am. Matthew had managed to pass out in the toilet which was overflowing with piss, sick and whatever else was in there. One of the boys shouted down the bus, "Anyone missing a son?" Vince came up the bus and carried him off while he was covered in crap.

All in all, a good day out. Hibs lived up to their reputation. We had a lucky escape in many ways. Hopefully, we'll play them again some day with a bit more than 48 hours notice next time. We gave a good account of ourselves this time and showed that even with little time to organise anything, we still had a fair turnout and a decent result.

Chapter 22
Cardiff C Squad
Alex Manning

The following story was given to me by a lad called Alex. Times have totally changed for these lads as CCTV is now in full action and trouble at football is no longer tolerated by Courts and the Government. As you will read, the numbers now involved in violence is down to dozens not thousands like in the 80's.
Annis

The C Squad is a name used by the Cardiff Youth firm over the past two or three years. In this time, it has seen the firm rise to one of the most active young firms in the country. Football violence for myself started in around 2001 and my first experience of battle was away at Bristol City in a game which was fairly heavily publicised and was used in a TV documentary a few years later. From that time, I have seen a seen a change in names and personnel associated with the youth element here. From a few of us 'tagging along' with older lads in the early days to the formation of the more organised 'Creche Squad' which was made up of young lads not only from various parts of Cardiff, but also from places as far as the east valleys, from towns like Usk and Cwmbran, from Pontypridd there was large number of lads and from as far a field as Carmarthen. The firm was relatively inactive compared to the last two years or so that I've seen though. We did travel frequently to various parts of the country where we were often stopped in our tracks by the all too familiar South Wales football intelligence officers. The few occurrences where violence did happen tended to be in 'suicide' missions including a game between QPR and Nottingham Forest where the away team were relegated. There were clashes between the fans after the game so three of us decided to have a look before being caught up in the melee. After backing Forest down the road with help from a few oaf-like Cockneys, we were turned upon by our new found 'comrades' who by now, had realised that we were certainly not QPR - our accents gave away that we were Cardiff. A few yardie types flashed steel and we were on the back foot. After a lucky intervention from a well known face at QPR (Gregors), we were given a pass on the understanding that we spread the word that this individual was still around and kicking! Further occurrences of this nature happened in Bristol and on other occasions in London as well as nine or ten of us fronting around 40 West Brom outside Sam's Bar in Cardiff on a Tuesday night where we were backed off but certainly not disgraced. We received praise from some of West Broms main lads regarding our efforts.

The C Squad came about over the course of 2005 with small pockets of young lads coming together to form the firm we have today. Personally I was just going with a few of my friends from the Creche days as many of the lads from that firm had drifted away for various reasons. There were many lads who I'd known from before but hadn't really bothered with in previous years as well as young lads who were just coming into the fold. This formed a good mix of lads between the ages of 16 and 21. We associate strongly with many of the older lads and are generally regarded by outsiders as just a part of the Soul Crew although we do try and make our own way in the football scene. We therefore regularly travel independently away from the older generation. Any lad involved in this way of life knows that when travelling away, the key to whether the day is a success or a waste of time is avoiding detection when getting to the town or city where your team are playing. More often than not, days have been ruined by the Old Bill collaring us before we've even crossed the English border.

One major time when we escaped detection and everything went to plan was in February 2007 when travelling to a league game at Coventry. After a few days of heavy snow and serious traffic disruptions getting on a minibus and onto the road was something of an achievement on this cold February day. After an early start, the perfect breakfast of lager and adrenaline soon lifted everyone's spirits as we made our way to the West Midlands. The journey was pretty straightforward considering the state of the roads after the bad weather and we arrived at Coventry in good time. We decided to settle somewhere on the outskirts of the city for the first part of our day and try to coax Coventry's firm into meeting us away from the bright lights and CCTV of the city centre. We ended up in a trendy bar in Earlsdon where we were bribed into behaving ourselves by the landlord who gave us free food and the odd free drink as payment for keeping his bar intact and his other punters happy. After numerous phone calls, it was clear that Coventry's 'Legion Youth' were unlikely to join us in our out of town location. After a few hours enjoying a few quiet beers and planning our next move, we decided to slip into a more central location. On noticing a public bus stop outside the bar, we decided to take this less detectable mode of transport into the city centre. Many of us had been to this city before and we knew our way around fairly well. We headed towards the main square in the centre of this dreary town. After having a quick look in a couple of bars, we decided to stop in a bar in Jordan's Well which is just on the outskirts of the city centre. On ordering my first pint, I heard a shout for us all to leave from one of the lads on his phone outside the pub. It turns out that Coventry had seen us pass through the city centre and had now followed us down Jordan's Well. We immediately began marching back towards the city centre and sure enough, marching towards us in the middle of a very busy road were 20 or so Coventry who appeared to be the youth element. We numbered 12 going into them but there was no way we had travelled here to give them a result.

The early exchanges were very violent. Punches and kicks came in from both sides as well as many items from roadworks on the pavement being used as weapons by both sides. Members of the public looked on in complete and utter astonishment and this prompted around forty emergency '999' calls to be made to police. The violence continued for what seemed like forever with a few lads taking a bit of a beating. One lad from Coventry was apparently knocked out at one point after running into a fucking lamp post! As the row dragged on, we backed them down the road slightly and, at one point, a few Coventry were on their toes. I believe to this day that, if it wasn't for two of their lads at the front holding their own, the Coventry mob would've been chased back into the city centre. One of these lads actually made a case to be selected for the England cricket team after catching a road sign flung by one of our lads in a manner befitting a world class wicketkeeper before making me dance out of the way of his return throw! Throughout the fight, a number of weapons were seen including knuckle dusters, batons and what appeared to be CS gas as well as various pieces of street furniture. Coventry eventually regrouped and came back at us chanting but this just encouraged us more. We again backed them off with the words 'Soul Crew' echoing around the street. Eventually the Old Bill arrived on the scene after finally getting through the mile-long tailbacks we had created. The sirens signalled everyone involved to disperse. About seven or eight of our group were rounded up near the scene and were stopped and searched under the Section 60 system. This would prove to be key for the police further down the line. Our own football intelligence officers were on the scene to make sure all information given by us was correct and after one arrest (for possession of a knuckle duster), we were ushered into taxis and sent on our way to Coventry's Ricoh Arena. Many of us at this point did not have tickets for the match and were therefore refused entry. Once police realised we were the same group that had been stopped earlier in the day, we were taken in riot vans and escorted to the train station where our minibus driver picked us up and we made our way home. The trip back to Cardiff was a lively one with everyone still buzzing that the row had actually gone to plan. Other than a few complaints about ripped Paul and Shark jackets and stained CP Company tops, the trip was basically a disco with The Stone Roses and the Twang providing much of the entertainment. All in all, at this time, the day was considered a success.

Other incidents involving our firm in recent times were away at Crystal Palace where, after a trip to London on the train, a chance meeting between members of the C-Squad and their Cockney counterparts ended in a violent encounter in Thornton Heath. It was a small incident numbers-wise with only seven or eight Palace lads involved against around ten young Cardiff. It was the outnumbered Palace lads who called the battle on though but inevitably numbers proved to be their downfall. They were backed off across the road. The incidents were fairly minor but still resulted in two arrests from the Cardiff contingent though both were eventually found not guilty which was good news all round. In the early months of the 2007/2008 season, the C-Squad was somewhat depleted with key members of the group being banned whilst on bail for the incident which occurred in Coventry. One game which did attract a turnout was Plymouth away, in part because it corresponded with our favourite Italian lunatics birthday! Though the lads bailed could not attend the match or go within a certain distance of Plymouth's Home Park ground, this did not stop a very violent incident occurring on the edge of the city where a few of Plymouth's older (and apparently main) lads were dealt a lesson that the phrase 'don't judge a book by its cover' is certainly true! After being confronted by around ten of Cardiff's young lads, they cockily laughed off suggestions that we could compete with them saying comments along the lines of 'good effort but we'll let you off this time 'cos otherwise you'll just get hurt'. With this, Cardiff steamed in and a violent battle ensued with a few minor injuries on both sides but the main blow being dealt to the ego of these Plymouth lads who certainly left with their tails between their legs. They were by no means bad but had seriously underestimated what was in front of them. There has been no action taken by the authorities in relation to this incident which is certainly good news for all involved.

Over the last few years there have been many other minor incidents worth a small mention. One of these was following an international game between Wales and Slovakia in Cardiff where a violent incident occurred involving members of Cardiff's youth element as well as many older heads. After the game, a number of Cardiff lads were gathered in a regular drinking spot in Canton when a group of around 25-30 approached who turned out to be Slovaks. The Cardiff lads inside the pub numbered about 30 and this 30 confronted the Eastern Europeans and immediately had them on the back foot. The lads from Slovakia did make a decent effort though but most who stood ended up taking a bit of a hiding before eventually being seen of by the local contingent. Another incident in which the youth was heavily involved was at the Carling Cup Final in 2007 between Chelsea and Arsenal. After meeting a lad I know from Chelsea for a quiet beer, myself and about 15-20 other youth lads were settled in a quiet bar in the city centre expecting to see a bit of an effort from one of the London firms but, unfortunately for us, none came. As the day went on, we ended up going into the same bars as many of Chelsea's main lads and even managed to bump into one of the main lads from Swansea who was meeting a publisher to discuss his recent book deal. As a non eventful day came to a close, a few of us headed back to our local pub and after many had left, we found ourselves confronted by approximately 25 Chelsea who backed us down the road and eventually dished out a bit of a beating to myself, another Cardiff youngster and one of our older lads, resulting in cuts, bruises and a couple of smashed windows! These were by no means Chelsea's top lads but they were certainly cockney geezer types intent on kicking fuck out of anything that came in their path.

Although there have been many incidents of banning orders being dished out to young Cardiff lads, serious sentences have been almost non existent. One major coup the police did unfortunately have in the last year was in relation to the Coventry City incident where five Cardiff lads were jailed for a total of 46 months with all convicted also receiving six year banning orders. CCTV and a lack of common sense and loyalty from two other lads involved (who incidentally managed to escape a prison sentence) conspired to allow the prosecution to have a very easy ride in convicting and sentencing us. After serving three months of a ten month sentence, I came out (as did the others) to a great reception from our older lads underlining the mutual respect we have for each other. I would also like to take this opportunity on behalf of all who were jailed to thank all who contributed to our release fund which paid for a very lively first weekend out!

Although banning orders and heavy policing limit the activities of both us and many firms around the country, success on the pitch resulting in an FA Cup final and potentially European football has certainly spurred the lads on and it would be naïve to say that football hooliganism in Cardiff will not continue long into the future.

Soccer thugs clas

VIOLENCE flared ahead of Cardiff City's game with Barnsley on Saturday.

Riot police and mounted officers had to deal with drunken brawling fans near Sam's Bar and Walkabout on St Mary Street.

Three men were arrested, a 26-year-old from Cardiff for violent disorder and a 35-year-old man also from the city for a public order offence.

A 33-year-old from Barnsley was arrested in connection with a drug offence.

There was trouble between rival supporters a number of bars in St Mary Street and police one bar was left badly damaged.

POLICE have launched an operation to catch the thugs who clashed when Cardiff City played Barnsley.

Operation Bolivia will seek to identify a hard-core of 50 football hooligans who took part in a spree of violence before, during and after Saturday's match at Ninian Park.

And detectives have released CCTV pictures of men they want to question about the trouble, with more stills expected over the next few days.

The violence started before the match when Barnsley fans began drinking from around 11am at Walkabout in the city centre. Cardiff City fans congregated opposite in Sam's Bar and windows were smashed and furniture damaged in both venues.

Officers moved quickly to deal with the violence but when it came to moving the Barnsley fans to the

ground, the g ted and a lar up St Mary S

Many sho caught up ir ance, during of violence police office keepers had their shutter

Once in the were furtl between the stewards an ficers also as

Detective C Graham Lloy CID, said a t ficers were wheedle out

"This is the ation in 12 I I've conduct quiries into liganism in said.

"We're munity-based

POLICE have issued CCTV pictures of men they want to question in relation to football hooliganism.

Operation Bolivia was launched after Cardiff City followers clashed with Barnsley thugs on February 8 this year.

A team of 10 officers has been working on the operation and so far 16 people have been arrested.

Of these, 12 have already appeared before the courts, with two cautioned, and two released with no further action taken.

Detective Sergeant Terry Lee said that the police had received an excellent response the last time CCTV stills were printed in the Echo and is hoping for more of the same again.

He said: "We were very pleased with the response last time and would now like to appeal for any information people may have on the four men pictured here."

The violence on the day of the Barnsley game began when opposing fans began drinking from around 11am at the Walkabout bar in the city centre.

Cardiff City fans congregated opposite in Sam's Bar and damage was caused in both premises, with windows smashed and furniture damaged.

Officers moved quickly to deal with the violence but when it came to moving the Barnsley fans to the ground, the group fragmented and a large number ran up St Mary Street.

Many shoppers were caught up in the disturbance, during which threats of violence were made to police officers and shop keepers having to pull down their shutters.

During the match itself the two sets of fans clashed again with stewards and police officers also assaulted.

If you think you know the men in these stills call the Operation Bolivia incident room on 029 2022 2111 extension 30195.

Hooliganism figures from Home Office

**Arrests at Cardiff games: 129
Cardiff fans' banning orders: 125
Arrests at Swansea games: 7
Arrests at Wrexham games: 11**

Conclusion

As you can see, even though our team for the last 30-40 years was shit and nearly always in the lower leagues and for years in the dungeon league (division 4), off the field, the Soul Crew were always in the Premier League.

As I said previously, the lads who wrote these stories were lads who I'd met through the years following Cardiff. It's in their blood and yes, it's 'over' due to banning orders, police intelligence and CCTV. But they will never take it out of them totally as it was such a big part of their lives. We get looked upon as major criminals but I preferred to mix with them rather than paedophiles, rapists, murderers, robbers and drug dealers. The media should name and shame a few more of those low-lifes and perhaps society would be a better place. The funny thing is that at the end of all this, a bond has been forged between us and we can now sit down and have a drink and a laugh about the good old days.

Personally I don't think anyone can really say that they had the best all time firm because, on our day, we all felt we were the best, from Barnsley to Chelsea. If the right lads meet the right lads on that day, fair enough but most of the time, for some reason or other, the Old Bill have at times arrived there first and stopped the mobs clashing, perhaps braking up one side's firm but then sometimes a battle still goes ahead and the firm that was depleted feel, in their minds, that they were never done.

No matter what other people say outside football, at the time be it the 70's, 80's or whenever, you felt you were fighting for or on behalf of your club. Unless people really have been there, they will never understand the buzz that there was at that time. Yes, of course we all get older, some take longer but eventually we all settle down and move on. I certainly have and enjoy my family life more than ever but, no matter what, they'll never take those memories away.

My follow-on book to this will be out next year. It is my own story from being a kid down Ninian Park to joining up with the original Soul Crew, my Court cases, from many battles away from football to my life in nightclubs which, on many occasions, was more violent than football ever was.

Annis Abraham Jnr

Other books by the same Publisher

Football Books

From Shattered Dreams to Wembley Way	Annis Abraham Jnr	£16.99 hardback
Ultras	Roberto Russo & Martin King	£14.99 paperback
Playing Up with Pompey	Bob Beech	£16.99 hardback
Gilly - Running with a pack of Wolves	Gilly Shaw & Martin King	£9.99 paperback
Bully CFC - The Life and Crimes of a Chelsea Head-Hunter	Gaetano Buglioni & Martin King	£16.99 hardback
		£7.99 paperback
Rangers ICF	Davie Carrick & Martin King	£16.99 hardback
		£7.99 paperback
Rivals - Fooball Fans Love-Hate Games	Martin King	£16.99 hardback
		£7.99 paperback
Blue Murder - Chelsea Till I Die	Mark Worrall	£9.99 paperback
Inside The Forest Executive Crew	Gary 'Boatsey' Clarke & Martin King	£7.99 paperback
Well Up For It	Simon Cheetham & Carl Eldridge	£9.99 paperback

Boxing Books

Harry Holland	Harry Holland & Martin King	£16.99 hardback
Blood, Sweat, Tears and Fears	Andy 'Stoneface' Till & Martin King	£16.99 hardback

See www.headhunterbooks.co.uk to order online or at all major Book Sellers.